Faith Fueled FINANCE$

A KINGDOM GUIDE TO FINANCIAL WISDOM & EMPOWERMENT

VERONICA ALSTON

Copyright @ 2025 Veronica Alston
ISBN: ISBN: 979-8-9919922-2-0
All rights reserved.

Author owns complete rights to this book and may be contacted in regards to distribution. Printed in the United States of America.

The copyright laws of the United States of America protect this book. No part of this publication may be stored electronically or otherwise transmitted in any form or by any means (electronic, photocopy, recording) without written permission of the author except as provided by USA copyright law. For permission requests, contact the author at the website below and/or through her social media handles.

Book Cover Design: SHERO Publishing
Editing: Synergy Ed Consulting
Graphics & Design: Greenlight Consulting
Publishing: SHERO Publishing

SHEROPUBLISHING.COM

VERONICAALSTON.COM

TABLE OF CONTENT

DEDICATION		6
INTRODUCTION		8
PART 1	*My Money Story*	14

PART 11-

Introduction	*Mastering Money*	48
Chapter 1	*Shift Your Financial Belief System*	52
Chapter 2	*Determine Your WHY*	58
Chapter 3	*Automate Savings and Investing*	64
Chapter 4	*Set Goals*	72
Chapter 5	*Eliminate Distractions*	78
Chapter 6	*Create a Freedom Plan*	86
Chapter 7	*Avoid and Destroy Debt*	94
Chapter 8	*Health is Wealth*	102
Chapter 9	*Faith Fueled Financial Living*	108

ABOUT THE AUTHOR- *Veronica Alston*   118

"True financial freedom begins when you align your money with your mission and your faith with your finances. Wealth is not just what you accumulate; it's how you steward God's blessings to create impact, purpose, and legacy."

— Coach Veronica Alston

Dedication

To my husband, Dan T., thank you for your unwavering love and steadfast support, that you have shown me and our family, throughout this journey. You have stood by my side, listening with patience, offering valuable insights, and helping us build a life together—spiritually, emotionally, physically, and financially. Your dedication and encouragement have been the foundation upon which this project was built. I am truly blessed to walk through life with you.

To our children, Daniel Jr., Olivia, and Lauryn, who make the A-Team complete: Being your mommy and bonus mom is the greatest honor of my life. You fill my days with light, joy, and purpose. My deepest hope is to leave you not only a legacy of love but also a spiritual and financial inheritance that empowers you to live boldly according to your God-given purpose. You will not have to start from scratch; instead, I pray you'll build upon the foundation of faith and finances we've laid and pass it on to your children. I love you with all my heart and am endlessly proud of each of you.

To my dear Mommy and Daddy, thank you for instilling in me the values of generosity and faith from an early age. You taught me the power of tithing and giving in alignment with God's Word, lessons I carry with me every day. Your wisdom has shaped my heart and my actions, and I am forever grateful for the enduring example you set.

To my family and friends, your unwavering support and encouragement have been a lifeline throughout this journey. Thank you for helping me transform swirling thoughts into words on these pages. Your belief in me, especially during moments of doubt, has been a source of strength and inspiration. I am deeply grateful for each of you and the unique ways you've contributed to bringing this vision to life.

In loving memory of my baby brother, Willie Lee Judon III, whose life was tragically cut short by gun violence as I was writing this book: Willie, your courage and refusal to let circumstances define you continue to inspire me every day. Your resilience and relentless will to rise above challenges are my greatest motivation. I honor your legacy with every step I take and every word I write.

And finally, to all Believers in Jesus Christ: My heartfelt prayer is that this book empowers you to take control of your finances and walk boldly in Kingdom economy. May it inspire you to live a life fueled by faith, aligned with the abundant blessings God has promised, and reflective of His glory in every financial decision you make. Together, let us step forward with trust, purpose, and divine wisdom.

Introduction

Thank you for picking up this book! I truly believe it has the power to change your life, but the real question is, *do you believe it will?* If you don't believe it yet, that's okay—just lean on my faith for now. Whether you're looking for ways to improve your financial situation or feeling overwhelmed, tired, or defeated, I'm here to guide you. Together, we'll break free from the paycheck-to-paycheck cycle and step into the abundant life God has promised. I believe in you, and I'll walk with you every step of the way.

Why *"Faith-Fueled Finances"?*

Because *without faith it is impossible to please God.* (Hebrews 11:6). Now, I know the subject of money, especially when tied to faith, can make some people uncomfortable or defensive. But let me be clear: this book isn't about money and the church—it's about money and God.

After over 15 years of providing financial counseling to both churchgoers and non-churchgoers, I've seen recurring patterns. Many believers misunderstand or have been misled about how to handle their finances, often relying on emotional appeals rather than Biblical principles.

You've probably seen it: a high-energy sermon where the preacher declares, "God is about to bless you with houses you didn't build!" or "Your blessing is on its way, so hold on to God's unchanging hand!" These words ignite what we call a "praise break," complete with hands clapping, feet stomping, pick 'em up, put 'em down, Holy Ghost good time. You are high-fiving your neighbor and everyone is caught up in the moment, filled with faith and hope for a breakthrough.

And when praise music slows down, the music shifts to something softer, gentler, that evokes emotion (the actual term for this is called *frisson*), the congregation is reminded to "bless God" and give so they won't be "cursed with a curse" according to Malachi 3. Driven by emotion, people give sacrificially, expecting a miracle. One lady shared that since she didn't have all of the money for her electric bill, she put it in the offering plate. When I asked why, she responded "I thought that's what you're supposed to do." Having faith, she put it into the offering plate, and guess what? The electric company shut her lights off. Wait a minute…. what happened? She believed during the service that God would bless her. I mean, she *really* believed. What happened between service and home? Did she not believe enough? Her bills were still there, no one called her to bless her with a house she hadn't built, her bank account was not overflowing, and she was still living paycheck-to-paycheck.

What happened?

Why didn't the financial breakthrough arrive? The answer is simple but profound: ***why would God bless us with more if we're not managing what we already have?***

This truth may be difficult to hear, but it's essential. Without addressing how we steward the resources God has entrusted to us, no amount of money will solve our financial struggles.

A Call for a Radical Shift

For years, I've seen too many believers struggling financially—not because God hasn't provided, but because they've overlooked the powerful financial principles outlined in His Word. Some pastors live comfortably while their congregants struggle. Others face financial hardships themselves, even filing for bankruptcy. What kind of witness does this provide to the world?

Sure, churches may have food pantries, benevolence ministries, and outreach programs that show their compassion, but are we equipping believers with the tools to manage their finances Biblically? Far too often, we see believers racking up debt, living for the moment, and praying for supernatural debt relief—all while neglecting God's financial principles.

I believe it's time for a **radical shift** in how we approach finances, both individually and as the body of Christ. The church must connect faith with action, providing believers with the Biblical principles needed to experience true financial freedom.

God's Financial Blueprint

The Bible speaks about money, possessions, and stewardship over 2,000 times. Ecclesiastes 10:19 tells us that *"money is the answer to everything."* Jesus Himself addressed money and possessions in several parables of the New Testament. This is no coincidence—our financial health is deeply important to God. Just as God, in His Word, has provided wisdom for how we speak, think, and live, He has also given us principles to help us handle our finances. From earning and saving to giving and investing, His Word offers clear wisdom and guidance.

My mission is to ignite a fire in Believers to embrace biblical financial principles that lead to freedom, stewardship, and abundance. This isn't just about numbers—it's about transformation. I want to see families breaking free from silence and having real, honest conversations about money, building a legacy of financial wisdom for generations to come. Together, we can impact the Kingdom in ways that go beyond our imagination, using our resources to glorify God and serve others. It's time to step into the calling of financial stewardship, unlock the blessings God has in store, and live with purpose, faith, and generosity.

This book will serve as your guide—a Kingdom Financial Compass to help you navigate a path toward abundance and debt-free living. Whether you're just starting your financial journey, drowning in debt, or wondering, *"How did you do it?"*—this book is for you.

Each chapter will provide step-by-step guidance, sharing the Biblical revelations and practical strategies that led me to financial freedom. If you apply these principles, I believe you, too, will experience a financial breakthrough.

A Journey Toward Purpose

I hope that, upon completing this book (and journal if purchased), you will not only discover God's financial plan but also feel empowered to apply it to your life. The reason? So, **you can fulfill His calling on your life without financial limitations**. God has uniquely designed each one of us with special abilities and purposes—no one else on this planet can do what you were made to do, in the way you are meant to do it. There are billions of people on Earth, yet God has uniquely crafted each one of us. Even identical twins have different fingerprints and purposes—each of us has been set apart to accomplish something specific, something only we can do.

As Believers, we must seek God's wisdom for managing our finances and resources, so we can operate effectively on this earth. Whether you are called to start a business, open a nonprofit, or write a book, applying the principles in this book will position you to fulfill your God-ordained destiny.

We, the Believers, can find all the financial wisdom we need in our manual—the Bible. Let's begin this journey together, trusting that with every step, you are moving closer to living a life that honors God and reflects His abundant blessings. Let this journey of financial transformation be a powerful step in living out the purpose God has set before you.

The Power of Journaling Your Goals

I invite you to embark on this transformative journey by reading this book and journaling along the way. There's a unique power in writing—it is not just a way to capture your thoughts, but a tool for healing and growth. I believe that when you see your own handwriting, it creates a deeper connection to your dreams, goals, and experiences. As you document your journey, you will solidify the Biblical money strategies we explore, going beyond simply reading or hearing them, truly making them your own.

Let's begin this journey together, trusting that every step brings you closer to living a life that honors God and reflects His abundant blessings. This journey of financial transformation is more than a personal goal—it's a powerful step toward fulfilling the purpose God has set before you.

KINGDOM GUIDE TO FINANCIAL WISDOM & EMPOWERMENT

VERONICA ALSTON

THE KINGDOM GUIDE TO FINANCIAL WISDOM & EMPOWERMENT

PART 1:
My Money Story

Part 1:
My Money Story

I learned the basic principles of money the hard way. I didn't grow up with a silver spoon in my mouth- my parents were what you might call, "upper-lower class." Our cozy 900-square-foot home in Kansas City, Missouri, was on 7th Street. It included three bedrooms, and two bathrooms, and housed five kids. Things were tight, but somehow, we made it work.

My dad worked as a machinist, and my mom stayed at home until I was in middle school. I was the middle child, with two older sisters who were 12 and 7 years ahead of me, and two younger brothers who were 2 and three years behind me. My brothers were just 13 months apart and often mistaken for twins. By the time I could remember much, my sisters were out of the house, so I naturally stepped into the role of the "oldest."

Our home was five blocks away from Wayne Minor Projects, a neighborhood filled with low-rise and high-rise buildings notorious for crime and gang activity. The crime was so severe that the government decided to dismantle the gangs by demolishing the high-rise buildings. Families were given notices and required to move out by a specific date. When the time came, the buildings were destroyed with dynamite. The demolition was unforgettable—our house shook as the buildings came crashing down. For many, it was a traumatic event; those buildings had been home to countless families. My Dad often said that everyone in Wayne Minor was "family." He had faced his own rough times but turned his life around after serving in the Army and finding Jesus, leaving behind a history of crime and gang involvement. While we didn't live in the projects, our connection to that world was undeniable. Poverty and crime were everyday realities.

Life at 708 Wabash was a yin and yang. We lived on the edge of poverty but never fully within its grasp. Our house stood just blocks away from neighborhoods marked by struggle, yet it was a place of stability and hope. My brothers and I would ride our bikes into those nearby streets, joining friends for games and adventures, aware of the challenges they faced but not entirely sharing in them.

Having a dad at home—alive, present, and not behind bars—was a rare blessing in our neighborhood, and we never took it for granted. While local schools were an option, my parents chose to send us to a private Christian school in our early years, where faith lessons shaped our understanding of the world. Sundays were for church, but the drive home often served as a reminder of the hardships others faced, as we passed streets defined by crime and struggle.

We weren't wealthy by any means. We had just enough to get by—no luxuries, no extras—but our lives were anchored by faith, family, and a sense of purpose that set us apart from the poverty surrounding us.

Home – Foundational Money Lessons

Money wasn't a common topic in our household. My mom rarely talked about it, but she quietly modeled financial discipline in the way she managed our household. She stretched every dollar, carefully budgeting to make ends meet. Grocery shopping was one of the few times I saw her handle money. She'd walk through the store with a handwritten list and never veer from it, paying with a check at the register. Every purchase was deliberate, every dime was accounted for.

Her actions spoke louder than words, showing me the power of discipline and resourcefulness.

My dad often talked about money, but it was clear we didn't have much. He'd point out how expensive things were and how tight the budget was, meticulously counting every cent and finding ways to stretch what little we had. I remember him involving us in small tasks, like sorting and rolling spare change into paper wrappers, showing us that every penny mattered. He also taught me how to read stock prices in the newspaper, often saying, "You can make money playing the stock market." Though I didn't fully understand it at the time, his careful approach to managing money and his belief in the potential to grow it left a lasting impression on me. My dad showed me that, even with limited resources, there was always a way to make money work for you.

Together, their actions painted a picture of financial survival—my mom stretching what we had to provide for our needs, and my dad constantly reminding us of the limitations we faced. It also gave me a sense of responsibility and a glimpse into how tightly they managed our finances. Though money wasn't openly discussed, it was always present in the fabric of our lives.

Around 9 years old, my Uncle Paul shared something with me that I'll never forget. Uncle Paul had schizophrenia, so our conversations were a little bit out of the ordinary at times. But on this particular day, his words stuck with me. He explained that everything in the world relies on numbers—even the chairs we were sitting in. He described how numbers are involved in measurements, angles, pounds of pressure, and degrees. He spoke with such passion, his eyes sparkling with excitement. Then he reached down to the ground, scooped up imaginary sprinkle dust, and tossed it into the air, saying, "Numbers are everywhere." At that moment, his words ignited something in me. I realized that numbers truly matter and are woven into the fabric of everything around us.

My grandfather, Willie Lee Judon Sr., also left a mark on my financial perspective. Grandpa was a determined young boy when he moved from Mississippi to Kansas City. With aspirations to serve in World War II, he told the recruiter that he was 18 when he was only 14. He made it to Europe but was sent back when the physician performing his physical examination determined that he was too young to serve. Returning to Kansas City, he worked on the railroad for many years.

Despite only having a 7th-grade education, he always seemed to have money. Every Easter, he gave us cash to buy new Easter outfits. Grandpa was a devout Catholic, burning candles and anointing us with oils he believed would bring blessings of wealth. The scent of his "money oil" lingered long after each visit and became a cherished memory.

Church – The Power of Giving

Then there was church. As a child, my dad would give us a list of chores and pay us $5 for the week. I'd take that money straight to Speedy's, the neighborhood liquor store, and spend it all on Now and Laters, Jolly Ranchers, and my personal favorite, dill pickles. But before we could go anywhere, Dad would always ask for a dollar back to put in the offering plate at church. It wasn't exactly 10%, but it taught me something important—always give.

One time, a visiting minister stayed with us, and when she left, she left $20 on my bed. I nearly passed out. That was a lot of money! I couldn't believe it. But instead of spending it at Speedy's, I did something different, I gave it all in church the next Sunday. The very next week, my grandfather gave me $40. That was my first experience with the principle of sowing and reaping, and it taught me the value of generosity.

School – The Banker's Lesson

In 5th grade, a field trip to Exchange City taught me an important financial lesson. Exchange City was a simulated city where each student was given a job for the day. You could be a teacher, fireman, gas station attendant, police officer, or mayor, just to name a few. I was the banker, responsible for managing the city's money- counting it, making sure everyone was paid for their work. It was exhilarating to see how money flowed and how people depended on it. That experience gave me an early appreciation for financial systems and responsibility.

The Young Adult Years – High School and College: Navigating Money Struggles

High school didn't bring many new financial lessons. I worked at McDonald's, earning just enough to cover gas and senior fees. Most of my focus was on sports and socializing, leaving little time for work.

The real challenges began before my senior year when my dad was diagnosed with bipolar disorder. His condition strained our family in every way. During his manic phases, he became unpredictable. During his depressed phases, he slept, a lot. To make matters worse, he was injured on his job and his employer let him go. This added great financial pressure to the family.

Throughout all of the turmoil, my mom had been working towards something bigger. During my 8th grade year, she decided to go back to school to earn her degree in computer science. My mom took on three jobs—teaching, cashiering, and selling oil paintings—to keep us afloat. Her resilience was inspiring. Without her determination and hard work, I don't know how we would have made it.

Despite all the hard work to keep us afloat, the household was falling apart. My dad's depression and erratic behavior, fueled by narcissistic tendencies, created chaos. He spent long hours either asleep or gambling at the casino, leaving no time or energy for anything else. The tension was strong between my parents and their marriage was hanging on by a thread. It was a heavy situation, and we were all exhausted.

College wasn't on my radar. It was expensive and my family wasn't in a position to help me with tuition or even provide much in terms of guidance. That all changed when my volleyball coach brought me applications and encouraged me to apply. To my surprise, I was accepted. When I told my mom, her response was simple: *"Go! There's nothing here, so don't come back."* Her words carried both exhaustion and hope, pushing me forward despite the uncertainty of how I'd afford it all.

Your Financial Foundation

Our early financial experiences lay the foundation for our values and influence the way we manage and spend money today. Conversations, decisions and even unspoken attitudes of those around us help form the starting point of our financial habits. If your childhood experiences with money were positive—characterized by abundance, careful planning, or financial security—you're more likely to have a healthy, balanced relationship with money today. You may approach it with confidence, view it as a tool rather than a source of stress, and feel equipped to make sound financial decisions.

On the other hand, if your experiences were negative—marked by scarcity, fear, or secrecy—those patterns can unconsciously follow you into adulthood. Perhaps you avoid financial discussions, overspend to compensate for past deprivation, or feel anxious about money even when you're doing well. These habits, whether helpful or harmful, often stem from lessons we didn't realize we were learning as children.

Understanding the root of your financial habits provides valuable insight into how your childhood experiences shape your current spending behaviors. These early influences often determine your mindset about money and the patterns you follow—whether consciously or unconsciously. By identifying these psychological influences, you can recognize and challenge unhelpful habits, replacing them with healthier, more constructive ones. For instance, you might work to shift from a scarcity mindset to one of abundance or learn to see financial planning as a tool for freedom rather than a constraint. Reflecting on your financial foundation is a critical first step toward intentional growth and building a more secure and fulfilling financial future.

College: The True Cost of an Education
Student Loans and Credit Cards

When my mom dropped me off at college, it felt like I was stepping into an entirely new world. For the first time, I was on my own. I was excited about my independence, but I had no idea how challenging some of the financial decisions ahead would be.

One of my first stops was the financial aid office where they explained my financial aid package. I had a partial scholarship for academics and track, along with a work-study job to help cover costs. Despite that, I still owed $5,500 a year for tuition. At just 18 years old, I didn't think twice about how to handle it. I took out student loans to cover the remaining balance, assuming it was the only solution. I didn't realize at the time, but this was about to have a long-term impact on my financial situation. Looking back now, I can't help but wonder: how is it that a teenager with no financial training can so easily borrow thousands of dollars—and what does that say about the system?

The Origins of Student Loans

The story of student loans is one of evolution, marked by shifts in priorities and policies that have shaped the system into the crisis we face today. It began in 1838 at Harvard College with the creation of the Harvard Loan Program. Funded by alumni and donors, this program aimed to help students afford their education, driven by a commitment to opportunity rather than profit. Harvard's model inspired other institutions, enabling many students to pursue higher education through community support.

In 1944, the federal government entered the scene with the GI Bill, which provided returning soldiers with direct financial assistance—not loans—to fund their education. This landmark policy underscored the belief that education was an investment in the nation's future. The focus shifted in 1956, when Massachusetts launched the first state-sponsored student loan program, catching the federal government's attention. By 1958, the U.S. began issuing loans for students in science and technology fields to compete in the rapidly advancing global landscape.

The true turning point came in 1965 with the passage of the Higher Education Act. For the first time, federally backed student loans were made available to all students, regardless of their field of study. While this expanded access to education, it also introduced a pivotal change: private lenders were incentivized to issue loans because the government guaranteed repayment. If students defaulted, the government recovered the money through wage garnishment, tax refund seizures, or other means.

What started as a well-intentioned effort to increase access to education gradually transformed into a system that prioritized ensuring repayment over supporting students. As college costs soared and borrowing became a necessity for many, student loans evolved into a financial burden that millions struggle to repay—a crisis rooted in the policies and priorities of a system that once aimed to help.

By the time I graduated at 22, I had $25,000 in student loan debt. While that might not seem like a lot to some, it felt like a heavy financial burden for a young adult just starting.

Credit Cards: The Hidden Trap of Easy Credit

Not only did I graduate with $25,000 in student loan debt, but I also found myself caught up in $2,000 worth of credit card debt. It all began when I encountered a table outside the financial aid office on campus. There was a credit card company offering an enticing benefit for a young, naive college student: sign up for a credit card and receive a free pizza. I didn't expect to be approved because I had no credit history, but I applied anyway—just for the pizza.

"Approved," the representative announced. Caught off guard, I asked, "Me?" He replied, "Yes, you, with a $500 limit." I was shocked yet proud. It was official, now I was grown, grown. Having a credit card was a rite of passage, a hallmark of adulthood. I couldn't understand how I had been approved, given that I had no credit history, a work-study job but no real income, and absolutely no financial knowledge beyond spending. Yet, I walked away with my pizza, a $500 credit limit, and a sense that I had entered the adult world. Unaware, I was stepping into a dangerous financial trap.

Initially, I hardly ever used the card, but over time, it became my go-to for "emergencies." I made the minimum payments on time but the bill never seemed to decrease. After about six months, I received a congratulatory letter praising my "good payment history," and informing me of an increased limit. Before I knew it, my balance had soared to $2,000—far beyond the original $500 limit.

Not fully understanding the trap I was in, I continued to make the minimum payments. While it gave the illusion of progress, the accumulating interest ensured that the debt kept growing. I never even considered paying off the balance in full each month; I didn't know that was the recommended option to avoid paying the 18.99% interest. I lacked the knowledge and tools to manage credit card debt effectively. The credit card companies, however, knew exactly what they were doing. Their goal wasn't to help me build a solid financial foundation—it was to keep me borrowing, accumulating debt, and paying more interest over time.

Reflecting on those days, I see how easily I fell into the credit card trap and how little I understood about credit cards. Those experiences taught me some hard lessons—lessons I wish I had learned much earlier. When you're young and just starting, it's easy to view credit cards as a pathway to freedom and independence. But without careful management, it can quickly become a heavy burden that's hard to escape.

Army Life, Marriage, and Debt: The Heavy Cost of Ignorance

After graduating with my bachelor's degree in biology, I was brimming with confidence. I thought I had everything figured out. I was young, energetic and ready to take on the world. Joining the Active Duty Army seemed like the perfect next step. I could gain new skills, travel the world, meet new people and get paid for doing it. Why not?

Meanwhile, my student loans from Sallie Mae and a growing pile of credit card debt weren't about to let me move on so easily. I had $25,000 in student loan debt hanging over my head, and each month, Sallie Mae came knocking. I'd receive their statement booklet, and like clockwork, I'd send the minimum payment. At the same time, I was chipping away at my credit card bill, doing my best to build a decent credit score. Then one day, as I was talking—mostly complaining—about the weight of my student loan payments to another Soldier, she told me something that sounded like music to my ears: I could go back to school, get my graduate degree, and my loans would go into deferment. Essentially, I wouldn't have to pay them back as long as I was in school. Without pausing to consider any long-term consequences, I applied, got accepted, and enrolled in graduate school. She was right, my loans were deferred, and Sallie Mae was on pause. My student loans were in deferment but quietly, the interest continued to accumulate, adding to the weight of my debt.

Feeling like I had outsmarted Sallie Mae by enrolling in graduate school, I decided to call the credit card company to see if they offered a deferment program like my student loans. The representative told me they didn't, but then hit me with a surprise: because of my "stellar credit," they were willing to bump my credit limit up to $5,000. *Sho nuff,* I was feeling on top of the world. You couldn't tell me nothing! $5,000? I might as well have had a black card in my wallet. Young and naive, I had no idea that a new cycle of spending and debt was about to catch up with me.

Cars: Appearance of Success

With my new credit limit in hand, I figured it was time to upgrade my life—starting with my car. It was time for a car that reflected my new "baller" status. I was in the Army, making steady money and working on my graduate degree. A new car seemed like the next logical step to match my "baller" image. I walked into a dealership and drove off in a 1998 Mazda 626. It was "money green" with peanut butter leather interior and a 6-disc CD changer. Oh yes! I was fly!

With no loan payments, a new credit limit and a beautiful new car, I thought I had it all together. But beneath the shiny exterior of my new car was a $13,000 loan with a 13% interest rate. I convinced myself this was a responsible, grown-up decision—far removed from the beat-up Ford Escort I had driven in college, purchased with student loan money might I add. I told myself that the new car was a symbol of how far I had come. But in reality, it was a reminder of how far I still had to go. I was adding more debt, convincing myself that each choice was a smart investment when in reality it wasn't. I was so focused on appearing successful that I failed to recognize the financial burden I was building, piece by piece.

Upgrades: The Price of Keeping Up Appearances

In 2002, my Army career hit a milestone—I was selected for direct commission as an officer. It felt like another opportunity to level up, not just in rank but in lifestyle. Continuing to feed my idea of what "baller" looked like, I told myself, *"You're an officer now; you need to carry yourself like one."* And in my mind, that meant trading in my trusty Mazda 626 for a luxury vehicle.

It was a 2002 Jaguar S-Type, sports edition. It was sleek, powerful, and everything I thought I needed to fit in as an officer. The price tag? $26,000. But that wasn't all. I also rolled over $10,500 from the remaining loan on the Mazda. Just like that, I had saddled myself with another $36,500 of debt.

Looking back, I can see how blinded I was by the desire to keep up appearances. The shiny car, the officer title—it all felt like proof that I had made it out of the "hood." But to tell the truth, I was living well beyond my means, chasing an image instead of securing my financial future. It was a dangerous game of appearances, and I was losing. I was so focused on projecting success that I didn't stop to consider the toll it was taking on my financial future.

The Personal Loan: A Reckless Decision

By the time I became an officer in the military, I had earned a new title and, apparently, a new level of "creditworthiness" with my bank. Out of nowhere, they offered me a $25,000 personal loan. I didn't apply for it, it just appeared on my screen when I logged into the banking app. There it was dangling in front of me like a carrot in front of Bugs Bunny. Did I need that kind of money? Absolutely not. Did I apply for it anyway? Of course I did.

The $25,000 sounded like a lot, so I convinced myself to only take $10,000. But here's the kicker: I didn't even have a plan for how to use it. The money quickly burned a hole in my pocket, and on a whim, I decided to spend it on a 10-day trip to China. I convinced myself it was a once-in-a-lifetime experience, and in many ways, it truly was. The memories were unforgettable—but so was the debt.

By age 26, I had accumulated almost $80,000 in debt— between my student loans, car loans, credit cards, and a personal loan. I was living in the moment, believing I deserved certain luxuries, without understanding the consequences of those decisions. It wasn't just about the trips or the cars or the material things— it was the mindset that led me to believe debt was the solution to achieving the life I wanted. My lack of basic financial education allowed me to borrow my way to the appearance of success, trading temporary pleasures for long-lasting financial burdens.

The Cost of Financial Illiteracy

Financial education is one of those things we often assume will come naturally, yet it rarely does. It's not taught in schools, hardly addressed in church, and usually overlooked on the job. In a world where money shapes so much of our lives, it's shocking how many of us are left to figure it out on our own— or worse, never figure it out at all.

I wasn't just financially illiterate; I was financially reckless. For years, I made decisions rooted in the illusion of success. I wanted to feel like I'd made it. But instead of building a solid foundation, I was digging myself into a deeper financial hole. I didn't understand the long-term cost of debt or how every swipe of my credit card, every car loan, and every indulgent purchase was chaining me to a future of financial stress.

I thought I deserved these things because I was working hard and sacrificing my life for my country. I didn't realize I was trading my financial future for temporary satisfaction. Each financial decision came with strings attached, and I was tying myself into a web I didn't know how to escape. It wasn't until I was forced to face my growing debt that I began to understand the price of my ignorance.

Married Life: Financial Struggles and Health Challenges

I met my husband, Chief Dan T. Alston, in South Korea in November 2007. He was a highly respected Soldier with a reputation as a go-getter. He was a recent graduate from the United States Army Warrant Officer Candidate School and his career was on an incredible upward trajectory. Despite his professional success, Chief's personal story was shaped by a tough, poverty-stricken upbringing. He often joked, "I grew up po, not poor—we couldn't afford the other 'o' and the 'r'." His childhood was a constant struggle to make ends meet.

Chief grew up in a four-room cinder block house with a tin roof. His family didn't have running water, and the only heat came from a wood-burning fire during the harsh winter months. There was no air conditioning in the hot and humid North Carolina summers. He and his family lived in rural isolation, so a car wasn't even necessary. Food was scarce, and during the summer, roasted peanuts were often his only meal. He walked through life with one pair of shoes that had to last him for school, play, and church—shoes that didn't always fit by the time the end of the year rolled around.

Chief's childhood was marked by financial trauma, isolation, and the kind of resilience that only comes from surviving tough circumstances. At 17, he saw the Army as his way out, and he never looked back. When I met him, I saw a man who had been through so much and still managed to rise.

Our story began in South Korea, where we quickly became inseparable. After Korea, Chief was stationed at Fort Liberty in North Carolina, and I was sent to Fort Riley, Kansas. The Army made it clear: you're either married or you're not. So, we navigated a long-distance relationship for a few months. In April 2008, during a weekend visit to North Carolina, we made a life-changing decision—we went to the justice of the peace and became husband and wife, less than six months after dating.

For Chief, the justice of the peace ceremony was perfect, but I still dreamed of a traditional wedding surrounded by friends and family. We planned a formal ceremony for June 28, 2008, but a month before our wedding celebration, everything changed. In May 2008, Chief began complaining of extreme fatigue and numbness in his legs. I remembered him mentioning similar symptoms when we were in Korea, but he hadn't followed up with a doctor. This time, I insisted he get an MRI.

His primary care doctor at Fort Liberty ordered the MRI, but before the results could be reviewed, the doctor was rapidly deployed. In the military, rapid deployments mean you're on standby, ready to leave at a moment's notice. For Chief, this meant his MRI results went unaddressed.

Two days before our wedding ceremony, Chief mentioned the fatigue and numbness again. I asked if he'd heard back from his doctor, and when he told me the doctor was deployed, I took it upon myself to check his results online. What I found left me frozen in disbelief:

"URGENT... SUSPECTED DEMYELINATION OF THE CENTRAL NERVOUS SYSTEM. IMMEDIATE REFERRAL TO NEUROLOGY IS NECESSARY. EMAILED RESULTS AND VOICE MESSAGE LEFT FOR ORDERING PROVIDER."

It was Multiple Sclerosis. My heart sank. We were just beginning our life together, and suddenly, we were faced with a diagnosis that would change everything. The weight of that moment was suffocating. We were newly married, living in separate states, and now grappling with the uncertainty of what this meant for his military career, his health, and our future.

It wasn't what I pictured when I said, "in sickness and in health," just a couple of months earlier at the justice of the peace. Those vows now carried a depth I wasn't prepared for and we were about to be tested in ways we couldn't have imagined.

I fought to get a change of duty station to be by Chief's side, but my unit was preparing to deploy to Iraq. The reality of balancing a serious health crisis, military careers, and a brand-new marriage was overwhelming. We were building a life together amid uncertainty, and the road ahead felt daunting.

Deployment and the Unexpected Gift

In September 2008, just a few months after our union, I deployed to Camp Liberty in Iraq while Chief remained at Fort Liberty in North Carolina. The physical distance was hard enough, but the emotional weight was even greater. We were living in two different worlds—separated by time zones, missions, and appointments—while trying to navigate the uncertainty of his health and the strain it placed on our new marriage. The stress was relentless, and we were both grappling with challenges neither of us was prepared for.

For Chief, managing a chronic illness while serving in the military brought unique struggles. For me, being away from him during this time felt like an unrelenting storm. I carried the guilt of not being able to physically or emotionally support him when he needed me most. And yet, despite his battles, Chief did his best to shield me from the weight of his challenges.

One evening, during a strained phone call, his voice carried a pain I had never heard before. "They're going to medically retire me," he said, his words heavy with defeat. "Why? There must be something else you can do!" I pleaded, my heart breaking for him. "I tried," he said quietly. "But they've made up their minds."

For as long as Chief could remember, all he ever wanted to be was a Soldier. His dream of serving began in childhood, inspired by his Uncle Herbert, who served in the Air Force. Chief spent a few weeks in the summer visiting Uncle Herbert, escaping the hot and humid summers. Those summers were an escape from the poverty and instability of his upbringing, offering him a glimpse of what stability and opportunity could look like. For Chief, the Army was more than a career; it was a promise of a better life. But after 13 years of service, his dream of a 20-year military career came to an abrupt and disappointing end.

As the reality of his medical retirement settled in, I sat with the uncertainty of what our future would hold. But one thing was for sure, I was not going to repeat the cycle of struggle I experienced with my dad's illness. My mother worked three jobs just to keep our family afloat, and I was determined to find a different path. I didn't know what I was going to do but I knew 3 jobs was not the answer for me.

Amid the challenges of deployment, there were occasional moments of unexpected joy. Care packages from charitable organizations, filled with snacks and toiletries, reminded us that our service and sacrifices were indeed appreciated. Special events featuring celebrities would also bring moments of levity. One such event occurred late in my deployment when Coach Bill Cowher, fresh off leading the Pittsburgh Steelers to a Super Bowl victory, visited Camp Liberty with other NFL coaches. The dining facility was beaming with excitement, especially among the Pennsylvania National Guard troops stationed alongside us.

A Soldier from another unit approached me with a unique request. He was heading out on a mission and couldn't attend the autograph signing. His son, a die-hard Steelers fan, dreamed of autographs from the coaches—especially Coach Cowher. Knowing I wasn't a Steelers fan (loyalty to my Kansas City Chiefs runs deep), he offered me a trade: if I went to the event for him, he'd give me a free financial literacy kit in return. "A finance kit?" I asked, intrigued but skeptical.

"Yes, it's supposed to help with managing money and paying off debt or something like that," he explained. Helping a fellow Soldier while surprising his son felt right. "Bet," I said with a smile, using our Kansas City slang for "deal."

I attended the event, collected the autographs, and kept my promise. In return, he handed me the Financial Peace University kit. I didn't immediately see its value, but in hindsight, that small trade would prove to be life changing.

As the deployment was coming to an end, I began listening to the CDs in the kit. The lessons on managing money, escaping debt, and building financial stability resonated deeply. It felt as though the messages were crafted specifically for Chief and me and the challenges waiting.

That kit became my "ram in the bush," a divine provision that set us on a path to financial freedom. What began as a simple favor became a pivotal moment. It was more than a transaction; it was destiny.

Gaining Financial Knowledge: A Journey of Hope and Vision
When Chief and I got married, money was not part of our regular conversation. We didn't have counseling or discuss budgeting. We operated on a simple belief: there'd be checks on the 1st and 15th, and that was enough for us.

As our unit transitioned home, I found myself with moments of stillness, moments where I could sit with my thoughts and face the growing uncertainty about our future. Chief's early retirement from the Army loomed large in my mind, and the reality of what it would mean for our finances started to sink in.

It was during those moments that I began listening—really listening—to the Financial Peace University CDs I'd received in that unexpected trade. At first, I was just trying to fill the silence, but soon, those lessons became more than background noise—they became a lifeline. The guidance on building an emergency fund, eliminating debt, and creating long-term wealth spoke directly to the fears and insecurities I had been trying to bury.

Every principle felt like a personal revelation. These weren't just financial tips; they were survival tools. With every track, I felt a spark of hope ignite within me. I began to see a way forward—a way to not only get us out of debt but to build a foundation strong enough to weather whatever storms lay ahead.

I binged those CDs as if my life depended on them because, in many ways, it did. Each lesson brought clarity and conviction. I realized that while Chief's health and career path were uncertain, our financial future didn't have to be. We could take control. We could rewrite our story.

To me, those CDs weren't just financial lessons—they were seeds of hope planted in the soil of uncertainty. And with every word, every principle, and every piece of advice, I began to cultivate a vision for a better future, one where financial freedom wasn't just a dream—it was a goal we could reach together.

The journey had begun, and along with it came a shift in my mindset. I wasn't just learning about money—I was learning about empowerment, about breaking cycles, and about creating a legacy. For the first time, I didn't feel like we were drowning. I felt like we had a plan, and that plan was going to change everything.

Taking the First Steps

From thousands of miles away, I called Chief. *"I've found something that will help us with money,"* I said, my voice filled with both excitement and urgency.

He listened patiently as I laid out the plan: we'd pull our credit reports, list every debt from smallest to largest, and tackle them one by one. Using my savings from deployment, I'd start chipping away at what we owed. Once we combined households, we'd live entirely on his paycheck while using mine exclusively to pay off debt.

Chief agreed, but he had one condition—he wanted to buy a house first. Owning a home wasn't a new dream for him. Even when we were dating, he presented sketches and floor plans of the home he envisioned. It wasn't just about having a roof over our heads; it was about creating stability, a place to build our future. He dreamed of a house with plenty of space, a primary bedroom big enough for a king-sized bed, and, of course, a "man cave."

When he told me, *"I don't want my wife coming home to a bachelor pad,"* I could feel the sincerity in his voice. I admired his vision, his determination, and his deep desire to give us a place where both of us could call home.

While I was overseas, Chief found the perfect home: a beautiful three-bedroom, two-and-a-half-bath house with perfectly manicured landscaping, red mulch lining the garden beds, and a bonus room that would become his beloved man cave. It was everything he'd imagined, and I couldn't wait to see it in person.

The Return Home

Coming home was bittersweet. In January 2010—almost two years after we'd married—I finally moved into our new home. It should have been a joyful reunion, a fresh start. But instead, it felt like we were stepping into uncharted territory.

I was 31, carrying the emotional weight of combat and the mental scars that deployment leaves behind. Chief, also 31, was facing a different kind of battle—coping with a chronic illness and the loss of his military career.

Our financial reality was starkly different than it had been during active duty. Chief's military pension was significantly smaller than his previous paycheck, and although he had secured a government contract job, his health made consistent work increasingly difficult. There were days when he'd come home utterly drained and other times when he'd have to leave work early because his body simply couldn't keep up.

Over time, his health continued to decline, and depression crept in. It was devastating to watch someone so strong and driven be slowed by invisible forces. Eventually, his doctor recommended him to leave work altogether and focus on his quality of life.

Financial anxiety

I was worried about Chief. He wasn't himself anymore—detached, indifferent, and weighed down by something I couldn't fix. It was as if the light in his eyes had dimmed, and his spark had faded. At the same time, I felt like I was carrying the weight of our finances alone. Anxiety crept in like an uninvited guest, feeding on every uncertainty I had about our future.

Financial anxiety isn't just about money—it's about fear. It thrives on the unknown, spinning endless *what-ifs* in your mind: *What if we can't pay the bills? What if we lose the house? What if things get worse?* My brain played these scenarios on repeat, pulling from memories of my childhood. I remember watching my mother work three jobs while my father battled bipolar disorder. She was exhausted—so tired that even when she was physically present, she was emotionally absent. My brothers and I were left to our own devices and some of the choices we made as teens reflected that absence.

I could feel history trying to repeat itself, but I refused to let it. I wasn't going to let money—or fear of it—become a wedge between Chief and me. I doubled down on my determination to secure our financial stability. I threw myself into the financial literacy CDs from *Financial Peace University* and began applying every principle I learned.

This wasn't just about paying off debt—it was about reclaiming control. My fight wasn't just for financial security; it was for us, for our marriage, and for a future where we wouldn't be servants to money or fear.

The Game Plan

Financial Peace University became the foundation of our journey to debt freedom. For the first time, I was hearing scriptures about money that went beyond tithing. Verses like Proverbs 22:7 hit me hard: *"The rich rule over the poor, and the borrower is slave to the lender."*

Debt... as slavery? I had never heard it put that way before. In my world, debt was normal. Everyone I knew had student loans, car payments, and credit cards. That was just how you did things—you borrowed money to go to college, you got a credit card to build credit, and you bought a car on payments.

But the way Dave Ramsey described financial freedom was different. He painted a picture of life without payments—without chains. He described the feeling of *breathing* when debt was no longer a constant weight on your chest. I wanted that feeling. I wanted that freedom.

Fueled by this vision, I sat down and wrote down a plan. I listed every single debt we owed, from the smallest balance to the largest, and prepared to tackle them one by one using the *debt snowball method*.

The strategy was simple but powerful:

1. List all debts from smallest to largest, regardless of interest rates.
2. Pay the minimum payments on everything except the smallest debt.
3. Throw every extra dollar at that smallest debt until it is gone.
4. Roll the payment from the paid-off debt into the next one, creating a snowball effect.

When I tallied our debts, the total hit me like a punch to the gut: **$389,000.**

It was a mountain of debt—student loans, credit cards, timeshares, cars, and a mortgage. And yes, I'll admit it: I had upgraded my 2002 Jaguar S-Type to a sleek 2010 Mercedes Coupe E-Class after returning from deployment. I liked cars—there was no denying it.

Looking at our debt snowball spreadsheet was humbling. Here's what we owed:

1. Sears Credit Card **$2,000**
2. Military Star Credit Card **$4,000**
3. Mastercard **$7,000**
4. Cadet loan 1 **$10,000**
5. Cadet loan 2 **$10,000**
6. Timeshare **$18,000**
7. Student Loans **$23,000**
8. Chevrolet Avalanche **$25,000**
9. Honda Accord **$34,000**
10. Mercedes **$43,000**
11. Mortgage **$213,000**

It was embarrassing to see over $100,000 in car loans alone. Lao Tzu once said, *"A journey of a thousand miles begins with a single step."* And for us, that first step was confronting the full reality of our debt.

It felt insurmountable—like staring up at a mountain peak with no idea how to climb it. But one thing was clear: I was determined. No financial hurdle, no health challenge, and no emotional barrier would stop us. Amidst these heavy challenges, we were determined to stick to the plan.

The first debt on our list was a $2,000 Sears credit card. It wasn't about the interest rate—it was about momentum. I needed a win, even a small one, to prove to myself that this plan could work.

When I made that final payment on the Sears card and highlighted it in green on my spreadsheet, it felt like I had cracked open a door to our future. That small victory fueled my determination to keep going.

In two months, I paid off our $4,000 Military Star Card. Then, I tackled the $7,000 Mastercard, clearing it in just over three months. Six months in, we had paid off three credit cards totaling $13,000. The momentum was building, and with every debt we eliminated, I felt lighter. For the first time in a long time, I felt hope—not just hope for our finances but hope for our marriage, our health, and our future. Debt had once been our prison, but step by step, dollar by dollar, we were breaking free.

Sacrifice for Success

Chief began to notice the momentum building. Every time I updated him on our progress, his interest grew, and soon, he was fully invested. Together, we leaned into the mission with everything we had, embracing a lifestyle of radical financial sacrifice.

We committed to live almost entirely on Chief's military pension—a fraction of what he had earned just a few years earlier. Every cent from my paycheck went straight toward debt repayment. Our date nights turned into free outdoor concerts, and dinners out became rare treats funded by gift certificates we received as birthday gifts.

We had a three-bedroom house, but realistically, we only needed two: one for us and one for my bonus son, DJ. The guest room became an unnecessary luxury, so we sold the furniture. Then we started looking around the house with fresh eyes. If it wasn't essential, it was sold—furniture, tools, décor, anything we didn't need. We quickly realized that building financial stability wasn't just about numbers on a spreadsheet; it was about facing our fears, leaning into knowledge, and working as a team. Every payment we made, every sacrifice we endured, and every plan we set in motion brought us closer not just to financial peace, but to a stronger, more resilient partnership.

It wasn't easy. Every decision meant giving up a convenience or a small comfort. No eating out. No frivolous spending. No "just this once" excuses. But every sacrifice brought us one step closer to financial freedom. Temporary sacrifice proved to be worth the exchange for permanent financial success.

At the end of our first year of intense focus, we paid off $33,000 in debt. The progress was exhilarating, a rush of hope that fueled our determination. But we also knew the road ahead was still long, and the sacrifices would need to continue.

Turning Setbacks into Comebacks

Our journey wasn't smooth—it was riddled with setbacks. Unexpected home repairs, surprise expenses, and emotional losses threatened to knock us off course. But every challenge became a reminder of why we started: to build a life free from the chains of debt.

One of the biggest hurdles was our $18,000 timeshare debt. It became a constant financial drain, with maintenance fees rising unpredictably year after year. After much prayer and reflection, we decided it was time to walk away.

We paid it off and then called the timeshare company to tell them we wanted out—completely. We didn't want to sell it, transfer it, or keep it in hopes that things might change. We were walking away.

At first, they were confused. *"Why would you give back something you've already paid off?"* they asked. It took days, escalations to upper management, and persistent conversations before they finally processed our request.

It was a $18,000 financial loss, but emotionally and mentally, it was one of our greatest victories. We knew keeping the timeshare would mean unregulated maintenance fees indefinitely, and even worse, passing that financial burden on to our children, just like the salesman had suggested as a "benefit."

Letting go of that timeshare was painful—no doubt about it. But it was also freeing. We had to forgive ourselves for making that financial mistake and then boldly walk away from it. That choice cleared mental space and financial resources for the next steps in our journey.

Miracles and Momentum

When we reached the $23,000 student loan debt, it was like deja vu, sitting at the base of another mountain. How could we climb this? How long would it take? The weight of it felt suffocating.

But then, God opened a door. At the time, I was no longer on active duty but serving part-time in the North Carolina National Guard. The Guard was short-staffed, and to encourage retention, they began offering signing bonuses. I signed up for an additional three-year term and received a $25,000 signing bonus.

After taxes and tithes, every single dollar went straight to that student loan. We didn't pause to celebrate or spend—it was deposited and immediately applied to our debt. That moment felt like a divine hand reaching down to pull us up the mountain. With the student loan eliminated, our confidence skyrocketed. Debt after debt began to fall, and with each payoff, our determination grew stronger.

When we reached the massive $102,000 in car loans, you would think that we would be intimidated but it was quite the opposite—we were an unstoppable force. Over three years, we cleared every single one of them.

Each payment was a victory—a declaration of freedom. Every balance we brought to zero felt like breaking another chain that had kept us bound for years. The momentum became our greatest ally, and the sacrifices no longer felt as heavy. With each debt erased, we could see the finish line getting closer. We weren't just paying off debt—we were reclaiming our lives.

The Final Stretch: A Journey of Faith and Freedom

Five years into our debt-free journey, we hit a milestone that felt like winning a battle—we became consumer debt-free, with only our mortgage left to tackle. The weight of credit cards, car loans, and student debt was gone. It felt amazing! We could finally breathe.

Soon after we found some surprising news —we were pregnant with Olivia. As a first time Mom I knew we needed to be closer to family. We decided to move to a new town and buy a new home. Instead of selling our first home, we chose to hold onto it as a rental property, believing it could be a tool for building wealth. But that decision came with consequences. Between the mortgage on our new home and the debt tied to the rental property, we found ourselves in **$500,000 in debt**. Yes, we were back in deep. And yes, we knew better.

For a few years, we tried to make it work. We managed the rental property, hoping it would become a meaningful investment. But eventually, we had to face a hard truth: Did we want to grow as landlords or live completely free from financial chains?

We chose freedom.

Selling our rental property was one of the hardest financial decisions we've ever made. Yes, we could afford both mortgages now that we were consumer debt free but deep down, we knew selling it was the right choice. Every dollar from that sale went straight into paying off our mortgage. It was the push we needed—the acceleration we had been praying for.

Again, we pressed, becoming laser-focused, cutting every unnecessary expense, channeling every extra cent toward our mortgage, and keeping our eyes locked on the goal.
And then, in December 2019, it happened.

The day we had prayed for, worked for and sacrificed for finally arrived. We made the final payment on our mortgage paying it off in 5 years and 11 months. For the first time in our lives, we were completely debt-free. No credit cards. No car loans. No mortgage. Every single thing we owned was paid in full.

The feeling was indescribable. It wasn't just about checking off a financial box; it was about stepping into the life we believe God always intended for us. A life of peace. A life of purpose. A life of financial freedom.

This journey wasn't a straight path. It was filled with detours, missteps, and moments when we felt utterly defeated. Some of the obstacles we faced were external—unexpected repairs, and financial surprises—but others were entirely self-inflicted.
And yet, through it all, God was faithful.

Philippians 1:6 became our anchor: *"I am sure of this, that He who started a good work in you will carry it on to completion until the day of Christ Jesus."* God started that work in us back in 2009 during my deployment to Iraq. At times, it felt like a boxing match—debt landing blow after blow, knocking us down over and over again. But every time we hit the mat; we got back up. Stronger. Wiser. More determined.

With each step forward, we realized that this wasn't just about us. This journey wasn't just about our freedom—it was about inspiring others to believe that financial freedom is possible. It was about equipping others to break free from the chains of debt and live the abundant lives God created them to live.

More Than Just a Financial Goal

When we started, we thought becoming debt-free was just a financial milestone—a finish line we could cross and call it a day. But when we reached the summit, we realized it was the starting line of something far bigger.

Debt isn't just numbers on a spreadsheet; it's a system. And as believers, we are called to live set apart from the systems of this world. Debt is one of those systems—a trap designed to keep us bound, distracted, and dependent.

The numbers don't lie. Over 80% of young adults aged 18–34 struggle financially, and more than half of Americans say that money negatively impacts their mental health.
But here's the truth: God did not create us to live in debt. From the very beginning, He has been our provider. He has always been our source.

A New Beginning

Now that we've walked this road, it's time to share the roadmap. This isn't just about avoiding debt—it's about building a life of purpose, peace, and abundance. It's about breaking free from the chains of man's system and stepping boldly into God's Kingdom economy. Proverbs 22:7 warns us plainly: *"The rich rule over the poor, and the borrower is servant to the lender."*

This book isn't just a guide—it's an invitation. An invitation to stop surviving and start thriving. An invitation to make bold decisions, to lean into faith, and trust God with every financial choice you make. Debt doesn't have to define your story. Freedom is waiting on the other side.

Let's take this journey together.

THE KINGDOM GUIDE TO FINANCIAL WISDOM & EMPOWERMENT

PART 2:
Mastering Money
THE BLUEPRINT

Introduction
Mastering Money

Although I've been in church practically my whole life, I had never been in a place where the pastor preached on Biblical financial principles. I'd heard all the powerful sermons about *faith*, *patience*, and *seed-time-harvest*, but what I didn't have was the *how*. I had faith. I waited for manifestation. But nothing changed until I opened God's Word and applied what I learned.

It wasn't until I was deployed in Iraq and received that financial literacy kit that everything began to shift. Listening to Dave Ramsey's perspective ignited something in me—a hunger to see what God's Word said about finances. I started digging into scripture for myself, and that's when it hit me: God has a financial plan for my life. It wasn't hidden or reserved for a select few; it was right there in the Bible, waiting for me to apply it.

I had faith. I believed. But James 2:17-18 became my reality: *"Thus also faith by itself, if it does not have works, is dead. But someone will say, 'You have faith, and I have works.' Show me your faith without your works, and I will show you my faith by my works."*

For so long, I had been crying out to God, expecting Him to miraculously *snatch me out of debt*. I wanted a supernatural blessing to erase my poor financial decisions. But God doesn't reward disorder. I was violating Biblical financial principles, mismanaging what I had, and failing to plan for my future. How could I expect God to bless me with more when I couldn't handle what He had already given me?

Stewardship Over Miracles

As we navigated the early years of our marriage, struggled through health challenges, and carried the crushing weight of significant debt, I began to seek God's guidance in every area of my life—including my finances.

Through my journey of studying faith and finances, I've learned a profound truth: God will not set us up for failure by providing us with more than we can handle. Sometimes, it's not a lack of opportunity or income that keeps us stuck; it's a lack of financial stewardship.

If we aren't managing what we already have with integrity and discipline, more money won't fix our problems—it will only magnify them.

But here's the beautiful part: God isn't withholding blessings out of punishment; He's waiting for us to be ready. He's waiting for us to align our financial habits with His principles.

Maybe you're not drowning in debt. Maybe your bills are paid, and your budget is balanced, but you still feel like you're not living up to your full potential.

This book isn't just about paying off debt or creating a budget—it's about stepping into the abundant financial life God has planned for you. But make no mistake—it's going to take more than faith. It will require applying God's financial principles with wisdom, diligence, and consistency.

The world's financial system is loud and persuasive. It tells us to borrow freely, live beyond our means, and focus on immediate gratification. But the Kingdom economy is different.

- *"The borrower is slave to the lender"* (Proverbs 22:7)
- *"Give, and it will be given to you"* (Luke 6:38)
- *"A wise man leaves an inheritance for his children's children"* (Proverbs 13:22)

These aren't just *nice quotes*—they're principles for living. They aren't designed to lead to fleeting success; they're designed to lead to generational wealth and a legacy that honors God.

Building a Legacy That Lasts

The dream isn't about *getting rich*. It's about leaving an inheritance—not just money, but a legacy of faith, discipline, and trust in God's provision. It's about creating a financial foundation that your children—and their children—can build upon.

When you manage your finances according to God's Word, you don't just experience financial peace; you experience spiritual and emotional freedom. You position yourself to fully walk in your God-given purpose without the limitations of debt or financial fear.

This journey isn't just about numbers on a spreadsheet—it's about transforming your mindset and aligning your actions with God's plan for your life.

In the chapters that follow, we'll dive deep into God's truths about finances. Together, we'll break down the eight essential steps to help you shift your financial focus and adopt a Biblically-Based Wealth Mindset.

You'll learn practical strategies to:
- Eliminate debt
- Build wealth with integrity
- Create a lasting financial legacy
- Operate within the principles of Kingdom economy

It's time to stop settling for less than God's best. It's time to rise above financial fear and step boldly into financial freedom.

Are you ready to take control of your finances and step into the life God has planned for you?

This isn't just a financial guide—it's a journey of faith, discipline, and transformation. Together, let's break the chains, rewrite our stories, and walk boldly into the future God has designed for us.

Let's begin.

THE KINGDOM GUIDE TO FINANCIAL WISDOM & EMPOWERMENT

CHAPTER 1
Shift Your Financial Belief System

CHAPTER ONE:
Shift Your Financial Belief System

Faith-Fueled Finances: Aligning Your Belief with Wealth

I have good news for you: God's greatest desire is for you to prosper in every area of your life. He wants you to thrive in health, flourish in your soul, and walk in abundance. In fact, He has a blessing with your name on it!

But here's the catch—God will only entrust you with more when you are faithful with what you already have. As Luke 16:10 reminds us, *"Whoever is faithful with very little will also be faithful with much."*

This isn't just about *managing money*; it's about aligning your mindset with God's truth about finances. Too often, people view money as a taboo subject—something discussed only in hushed tones when gas prices rise or grocery bills climb. But rarely do we discuss money in a positive, empowered light.

I'm here to change that! My goal is to have Believers boldly talking about money, embracing it not as something to fear, but as a tool and resource God has entrusted to us. It's time to shift our thinking and begin to view money from a Kingdom perspective.

God's Kingdom Economy

Nothing in life happens without money, yet so few of us are taught how to handle it. Schools don't teach it. Churches often shy away from discussing it—other than during tithes and offerings. Friends and family rarely bring it up. And as a result, many of us grow up with distorted beliefs about money—seeing it as a *barrier* rather than the *blessing* God intended it to be. But here's the truth: **Money isn't the problem. Our beliefs about money are.**

If you think of money as something you'll *never have enough of*, that belief becomes your reality. But if you see money as a resource entrusted to you by God to fulfill His purposes, you unlock the potential to live a life of freedom, purpose, and impact.

To fully understand God's perspective on wealth, we need to return to Genesis, to the very beginning. Before creating Adam, God prepared everything mankind would need to thrive—food, water, trees, animals, and even gold and silver, which later became symbols of trade and wealth.

His first command to Adam and Eve was: *"Be fruitful and multiply; fill the earth and subdue it"* (Genesis 1:28). God's intention was clear: Humanity was to manage, cultivate, and steward the resources He provided. This command established God's economy—a system rooted in abundance and stewardship. In the Garden of Eden, Adam and Eve lacked nothing. Their needs were met effortlessly.

It was only after disobedience entered the picture that resources became harder to obtain. But even then, God's command to steward the earth remained. His Kingdom economy is still in effect today, and we are called to align with it.

Shifting Your Beliefs About Money

Money doesn't have to be a *touchy subject*. In fact, when Jesus taught His disciples to pray, He said, *"Your kingdom come, Your will be done, on earth as it is in heaven"* (Matthew 6:10).

Heaven operates without lack, debt, or scarcity. And God's will is for His Kingdom principles to be reflected here on earth—including in our finances.

But before we can align our financial habits with Kingdom principles, we must shift our financial belief system.

Many people carry false beliefs like:

- ☐ *"I'll always have debt."*
- ☐ *"I'll always have a car payment."*

These are myths rooted in worldly systems, not Kingdom truths. The Bible says, *"As a man thinks in his heart, so is he"* (Proverbs 23:7).

If you believe you'll always struggle financially, that belief will shape your reality. To walk in financial freedom, we must adopt three foundational beliefs based on God's Word:

1. Believe You Are Blessed

From the very beginning, God blessed humanity. *"So, God created mankind in His own image... God blessed them"* (Genesis 1:27-28). You are blessed because you were made in God's image. This isn't just a feel-good statement; it's a Kingdom truth.

Being blessed doesn't mean life will be free of struggles. It means you have God's favor, grace, and divine benefits:

- ☐ Material blessings like financial prosperity and health.
- ☐ Spiritual blessings like love, joy, peace, and self-control.

Being blessed means you can face life's challenges with strength, hope, and clarity. You can live a life of purpose and fulfillment, knowing God's favor rests upon you.

2. Believe You Have Everything You Need

In God's economy, there is no lack. *"My God will meet all your needs according to the riches of His glory in Christ Jesus"* (Philippians 4:19). God has already equipped you with everything you need to fulfill your purpose.

Even when it doesn't *feel* like it—when resources seem scarce or opportunities feel distant—His Word is unchanging. *"For you created my inmost being; you knit me together in my mother's womb. I praise you because I am fearfully and wonderfully made"* (Psalms 139:13-14).

3. Believe Wealth Is a Gift

Wealth is not something to fear or resent; it is a gift from God. *"Moreover, when God gives someone wealth and possessions, and the ability to enjoy them, to accept their lot and be happy in their toil—this is a gift of God"* (Ecclesiastes 5:19).

Wealth isn't about greed or selfishness. It's about using the resources God entrusts to you to bless others, advance His Kingdom, and glorify His name.

What Is True Wealth?

Wealth is more than money. It's freedom—freedom from debt, freedom from stress, and freedom to fully pursue God's calling on your life.

True wealth includes:

- ☐ Physical health
- ☐ Emotional well-being
- ☐ Spiritual peace

God is our ultimate provider. He has given us the *power to create wealth* (Deuteronomy 8:18) and the wisdom in His Word to steward it well.

When we align our beliefs with God's Word, we start to see opportunities instead of obstacles. Challenges become moments of growth. Our mindset shifts from scarcity to abundance.

Change doesn't happen overnight. But as we speak life into our finances and manage money according to Kingdom principles, we begin to experience the abundance God has promised. Your belief is the most powerful attribute you possess.

Let's believe God, speak life over our finances, trust His promises, and watch Him transform our financial lives for His glory.

CHAPTER 2

Fuel Your Financial Journey with Purpose

CHAPTER TWO:
Determine Your WHY- Fuel your Financial Journey with Purpose

Congratulations! You've embraced the truth that wealth is not only possible but part of God's design for your life—a gift entrusted to you for a greater purpose. Now, it's time to dig deeper and uncover the heartbeat of your financial journey: your "why."

Your *"why"* isn't just a goal—it's your purpose. It's the unwavering reason that keeps you moving forward, even when the road gets tough. It's the driving force behind the sacrifices you'll make, the discipline you'll cultivate, and the resilience you'll need to pursue your God-given financial destiny.

A strong *"why"* isn't optional—it's essential. It's the secret weapon that empowers you to say no to fleeting desires and yes to God's greater vision for your life.

Obstacles are inevitable, but with a God-centered "why," no challenge is insurmountable. When your purpose is rooted in God's promises, you'll discover a strength within yourself that can only come from Him.

The Power of a Clear Purpose

There's something miraculous about what people can achieve when they are deeply connected to their purpose. We've all heard stories of people accomplishing impossible tasks in moments of urgency—like a parent lifting a heavy object to save their child or someone running into a burning building to rescue a loved one. These acts aren't just about physical strength—they're fueled by unshakable purpose, love, and urgency.

Thankfully, your financial journey doesn't require extraordinary stunts or heroic acts. Yet, the principle remains the same: the power you need to succeed lies within you, placed there by God Himself.

Genesis 1:28 reminds us that we are made in God's image. That means we are equipped with His creative power, and everything we need to achieve our purpose is already inside of us. But unlocking that power and potential requires intention, action, and an unshakable understanding of your "why."

Discovering My Why

Your *"why"* is deeply personal—it's as unique as your fingerprint. I can't define it for you, but I can share my own.

As an African American woman, my family's history is one of resilience and overcoming systemic challenges. For over 400 years, African Americans have faced oppression, segregation, and limited financial resources. Each generation has fought tirelessly to build a better future, but far too often, we've had to start from scratch. For my bloodline, that cycle stops with me!

My *"why"* is to break this generational pattern and create a legacy of financial freedom and opportunity for my family. I don't just want my children to survive—I want them to thrive.

If my daughter dreams of becoming a dentist and owning her own practice, I want to do more than pay for her education—I want to buy the building where she'll fulfill her calling.

But this dream isn't just about money—it's about obedience to God's Word.

Proverbs 13:22 reminds us: *"A good man leaves an inheritance to his children's children, but the wealth of the sinner is stored up for the righteous."* And 1 Timothy 5:8 declares: *"Anyone who does not provide for their relatives, and especially for their own household, has denied the faith and is worse than an unbeliever."*

For me, inheritance and provision go beyond financial stability—they mean ensuring that I provide for my family. My *"why"* is about creating opportunities that enable my children—and future generations—to walk in their God-given purposes without financial barriers.

A Legacy Mindset

When I think about legacy, I'm reminded of people like David Steward, the founder of Worldwide Technology. Born during segregation in Missouri, David Steward overcame immense challenges to become one of the wealthiest African Americans in the United States. But his success wasn't just about personal wealth—it was about creating opportunities for others and inspiring future generations. As Steward once said: *"We have a personal obligation to help the next generation."*

Proverbs 22:6-7 offers a profound blueprint for legacy: *"Train up a child in the way he should go, and when he is old, he will not depart from it. The rich rule over the poor, and the borrower is slave to the lender."*

These verses, placed side by side, show us a powerful connection:
- ☑ Teach your children wisdom about finances.
- ☑ Equip them to avoid debt and embrace God's principles of stewardship.

Experience is the best teacher, and I want my children to learn not just from my words but from my example.

My *"why"* drives me to ensure that no generation in my family ever has to start from scratch again.

What's Your Why?

Your *"why"* is the fuel that will keep you moving forward when the journey feels uphill. It will anchor you during seasons of uncertainty and strengthen your resolve when distractions come your way.

Whether your *"why"* is about:

- ☐ Breaking generational cycles
- ☐ Creating opportunities for your children
- ☐ Fulfilling a God-given vision

…it's crucial to stay connected to it.

When you align your "why" with God's will, you'll find the motivation and endurance to keep going. And as you press forward, you'll witness the miraculous power of God working through you—not just to transform your finances, but to create a ripple effect that touches lives and advances His Kingdom.

Hold your Why close. Write it down. Meditate on it. Pray over it. Let your *"why"* guide your decisions, inspire your actions, and keep you focused on God's greater vision.

With a faith-fueled "why," there is nothing you cannot achieve. Let your purpose be the spark that ignites your journey to financial freedom and Kingdom impact.

THE KINGDOM GUIDE TO FINANCIAL WISDOM & EMPOWERMENT

CHAPTER 3

Automate Savings & Investing

CHAPTER THREE:
Automate Savings & Investing

Breaking Free from Man's Economy: Embracing Kingdom Principles

The enemy's plan is clear: to keep you trapped in financial chaos, living paycheck to paycheck, and feeling overwhelmed by debt and scarcity. This state of constant financial struggle isn't just inconvenient—it's a spiritual trap designed to keep you unproductive and ineffective in the Kingdom of God.

But God has a better plan for your finances. He calls us to live under a Kingdom economy—a divine system established from the foundation of the earth. Unlike man's economy, which is driven by fear, greed, and debt, the Kingdom economy is rooted in trust, abundance, and stewardship. To break free from financial bondage, we must identify the enemy's traps, reject his tactics, and embrace God's principles.

The Enemy's Tactics: Keeping You in Financial Bondage

Satan, the prince of this world, thrives on keeping people in financial chaos. When we're stuck living paycheck to paycheck, it's hard to focus on generosity, ministry, or long-term goals. The enemy's traps are subtle but effective:

- **Impulse Spending:** Temptation to prioritize fleeting pleasures over lasting security.
- **Scarcity Thinking:** Lies of lack that convince us we can't afford to save or invest.
- **Distractions and Clever Marketing:** Constant bombardment of ads that pull us away from wise financial decisions.

The result? Financial chaos, stress, and a lack of fruitfulness in God's Kingdom. As Joseph Sangle, a biblical financial expert, reminds us: ***"If the devil can keep you broke, he can keep you ineffective."***

But this is not God's design. Living a faith-fueled, financially abundant life requires us to live in a Kingdom economy. It demands discipline, trust in God's principles, and intentional action. By following God's principles, you can break free and step into financial freedom. There are two main steps you must take:

Step 1: Acknowledging God Through Tithing

Let's be honest: tithing is often misunderstood. Many people view it as an obligation rather than an opportunity to declare trust in God's provision. The truth is, tithing isn't about God needing your money—He owns everything: *"The earth is the Lord's, and everything in it"* (Psalm 24:1). Tithing is foundational to Kingdom living; it's an act of faith and obedience. It declares that you trust God's provision and honor Him as the source of all your resources. Tithing is a bold statement. It acknowledges that God can do more with 10% than we ever could do with 100%.

Proverbs 3:9 tells us, *"Honor the Lord with your wealth, with the first fruits of all your crops."* Tithing aligns us with God's principles and keeps our priorities in check.

Tithing says:
- ☑ *"God, I trust You."*
- ☑ *"God, You are my priority."*
- ☑ *"God, I honor You with the first fruits of my labor."*

Now, let's pause to address a common question: *Do you tithe on your gross income or your net income?* My pastor, Dr. Jeffery Chapman Sr., once asked, "Do you want God to bless you on the gross or the net?" That settled it for me—I tithe on the gross. If you're unsure where to start, just start where you are and honor God with your first fruits. This act of faith will align your finances with God's principles and open the door to His provision.

Step 2: Acknowledging Yourself Through Saving and Investing

Many people neglect themselves financially, prioritizing bills and obligations over savings and investments. This pattern leaves nothing for the future and reflects poor stewardship. When people tell me that they don't have enough money left over to save or invest I often offer this suggestion: "Perhaps your budget is upside down." To break the cycle of "not enough" adopting this simple yet profound Kingdom principle can position you to experience God's design for stewardship and cultivate lasting financial success: pay yourself first.

When you pay yourself first you prioritize your financial future by setting aside resources for your future before anything else and it helps you break free from the traps of living paycheck to paycheck.

Paying yourself first isn't just a financial habit—it's a bold declaration that you will not let fear, distractions, or marketing ploys rob you of the abundant life God has promised. When you pay yourself first, you are reclaiming control of your finances and declaring that you trust God's provision over the enemy's lies. This act of faith positions you to experience the abundance of Kingdom economy and you will begin to see the manifestation of God's financial plan for your life.

The Importance of Saving and Investing

Consider these staggering facts:

- The Federal Reserve reported in 2023 that over 37% of Americans couldn't cover a $400 emergency.
- Bankrate revealed that 27% of Americans have no savings at all.

Saving and investing create financial stability, helping you prepare for emergencies and future opportunities. Saving and investing are not just practical—they're biblical. The Bible provides powerful examples of how these principles pay off:

- **Joseph in Egypt** (Genesis 41): Joseph's strategy of storing grain during seven years of abundance ensured survival during seven years of famine. His foresight saved nations.
- **The Parable of the Talents** (Matthew 25:14-30): The servants who multiplied their master's resources were praised, while the one who buried his talent out of fear was rebuked. This story highlights the importance of growth and stewardship.

By saving and investing, you're not only building financial security but also positioning yourself to be a blessing to others.

How to Break the Cycle: Practical Steps

1. **Treat Savings and Investing Like Bills**
   Savings and investments should be non-negotiable—just as important as rent or utilities. Automate these contributions to ensure consistency.

2. **Start Small and Be Consistent**
   - Save at least 10% of your income.
   - If your employer offers a retirement match, invest enough to get the full match. If not, start with as little as $50 per month.
   - Consistency is key; even small amounts add up over time.

3. **Build an Emergency Fund**
   Focus first on saving 3-6 months' worth of living expenses in an easily accessible account. This provides a safety net for unexpected challenges.

4. **Automate Your Finances**
   Automation is a game-changer. Set up automatic transfers to savings and investment accounts. This "out of sight, out of mind" approach reduces temptation and ensures your financial plan stays on track.

5. **Use Tools and Apps**
   Leverage financial apps or banking tools to schedule recurring transfers.

Building Your Financial Muscle

Remember, breaking free from financial bondage is a journey. Building your savings and investing muscle takes time and discipline. Consistency, not perfection, is what creates lasting results. Every dollar you save and invest is a step toward financial freedom and Kingdom impact.

Preparing for the Next Step

Tithing, savings and investing are not optional, they are foundational habits that position you to experience God's blessings. With your tithing, savings, and investments automated, you're now ready to create a budget for the rest of your money. Budgeting is a powerful tool for managing expenses, eliminating debt, and aligning your spending with God's purpose for your life. In the next chapter, we'll explore how to craft a Kingdom-focused budget that empowers you to live abundantly and give generously.

Your journey to financial freedom is just beginning. By embracing these principles and trusting God's plan, you're taking bold steps toward a life of purpose, provision, and impact. Let's continue this journey together.

THE KINGDOM GUIDE TO FINANCIAL WISDOM & EMPOWERMENT

CHAPTER 4
Set Financial Goals

CHAPTER FOUR:
Set Financial Goals

Be a Goal Getter!

"For I know the plans I have for you," declares the Lord, "plans to prosper you and not to harm you, plans to give you hope and a future." – **Jeremiah 29:11**

Have you ever considered that God has already mapped out extraordinary plans for your life? These aren't just ordinary plans—they are divinely crafted blueprints, designed with purpose, prosperity, and fulfillment in mind. The dreams nestled in your heart are not random; they are whispers from heaven, lovingly placed within you by the Creator Himself.

When God shaped your eyes, He envisioned the extraordinary things you'd see. When He fashioned your ears, He prepared them to hear moments of inspiration that would transform your life. God is constantly whispering, constantly planting seeds in the soil of our destiny. So don't shrink back from the dreams God has placed in your heart. They are not too big, too distant, or too impossible—they are divine invitations to step into the abundant life He has prepared for you.

Why Set Financial Goals?

Before embarking on any journey, you must first know your destination. Without a clear goal, you risk wandering aimlessly. Setting financial goals is like placing coordinates into your spiritual and financial GPS. Goals provide clarity, focus, and direction.

After reading this chapter, I pray your financial goals will include: demolishing debt, achieving peace of mind, building generational wealth, and living a life of generosity and purpose. These are not pie-in-the-sky fantasies—they're tangible, God-ordained visions.

Now, let's dream for a moment. Close your eyes and take a deep breath. If money were no obstacle, what would you do with your life? Would you stay where you are or would you pursue the dreams buried deep within you?

If your answer is to continue your current path, you are aligned with your God-given purpose. But if your heart whispers for more—if it tells you to leave behind the familiar and step into the extraordinary—then it's time to realign your path with God's plan.

Understanding your purpose begins with asking:

- ☑ What do you love?
- ☑ What are you passionate about?
- ☑ What brings you fulfillment?

When you discern God's purpose for your life, you can create purpose-driven goals. Financial freedom is not just about accumulating wealth—it's about positioning yourself to fulfill God's will without limitations.

The Power of Goals: Vision and Direction

"Where there is no vision, the people perish, but he that keepeth the law, happy is he." Proverbs 29:18.

Vision is the spark that ignites your future. It's what propels you forward when circumstances feel overwhelming.

Goals bring clarity to your vision serving as a roadmap to your destination. Without them, it's easy to lose focus, but with them, you gain purpose, direction, and the courage to persevere.

Vision: Create Your Vision Board

A vision board is a powerful way to turn your aspirations into tangible reminders of God's promises. Gather images, quotes, and scriptures that represent your dreams—whether it's people you wish to impact, places you want to explore, or things you hope to achieve. Use it as a daily reminder of the life He has called you to live.

1. People

Who are the people God has called you to inspire and bless? Perhaps it's your family, your community, or those you have yet to meet. Place their images or symbols on your board as reminders of the lives you are working to impact. *(For me, that's the Alston and Judon namesake and Believers all over the world.)*

2. Places

Visualize the places God is calling you to—whether for rest, learning, or serving. Just as God called the Israelites to take possession of their promised land *(Deuteronomy 1:8)*, He has territories for you to claim.

3. Things

There's no shame in desiring material blessings when they align with God's purpose. *2 Corinthians 9:8* tells us, *"God is able to bless you abundantly, so that in all things at all times, having all that you need, you will abound in every good work."*

Dream big—whether it's a home, a business, or resources to bless others, dream big. *Now to Him who is able to do exceedingly abundantly above all that we ask or think, according to the power that works in us.* Ephesians 3:20

Direction: Your Roadmap to Success

Vision alone isn't enough—you need direction to get there. Goals serve as your step-by-step plan, ensuring you stay the course. To achieve financial success, set both short-term and long-term goals. Use the SMART method to transform your dreams into actionable steps:

SMART Goals

1. **Specific:** Be clear about what you want to achieve. Instead of saying, *"I want to save money,"* say, *"I will save $10,000 for a down payment for a house."*

2. **Measurable:** Define how you'll track progress. Saving $500 a month for 20 months is measurable and achievable.

3. **Achievable:** Set goals that challenge you but remain realistic.
Trust that *"I can do all things through Christ who strengthens me"* (*Philippians 4:13*).

4. **Relevant:** Ensure your goals align with God's purpose for your life.
Ask yourself, *"Is this the right season?"*

5. **Time-bound:** Assign a deadline to your goals.
☐ *"I will save $10,000 by April 2027."*

SMART Goal Example:

"I will save $500 a month for 20 months ($10,000) for a down payment on a house by April 1, 2027, to achieve my goal of homeownership by age 25. I will automate these savings directly from my paycheck."

This goal is Specific, Measurable, Achievable, Relevant, and Time-bound—a plan that is both practical and rooted in biblical wisdom.

Triumph Through Discipline

Achieving your financial goals will require stepping out of your comfort zone. Remember, no Olympic champion rises to greatness by staying comfortable. They train tirelessly, endure challenges, and persevere through setbacks because their vision drives them forward.

Similarly, financial discipline demands effort and perseverance. But when your plans align with God's purpose, no challenge is insurmountable. As Proverbs 16:3 reminds us, *"Commit to the Lord whatever you do, and He will establish your plans."*

Dream Boldly. Plan Wisely. Trust Fully.

With God as your guide, your financial goals will lead you into a future more abundant than you can imagine. As Zig Ziglar once said: "A goal properly set is halfway reached." Your journey starts now. Set your goals, trust God with every step, and watch Him do exceedingly, abundantly above all you could ask or think. The path to triumph is before you—step into it with faith and purpose!

THE KINGDOM GUIDE TO FINANCIAL WISDOM & EMPOWERMENT

CHAPTER 5
Eliminate Distractions

CHAPTER FIVE
Eliminate Distractions

This chapter will challenge and inspire you, so get ready! Over the years, I've counseled countless people on their financial journeys, and I discovered a recurring obstacle that often derails their progress: **distractions**.

Distractions are anything that takes your focus away from achieving your goals. They don't always show up in obvious or dramatic ways. In fact, many distractions are as subtle, sneaking into your mind quietly, much like the serpent in the Garden of Eden.

When Satan spoke to Eve, he shifted her focus from God's promises. In the same way, financial distractions can shift our focus away from God's promise in *Deuteronomy 8:18*, which says, *"But remember the Lord your God, for it is He who gives you the ability to produce wealth, and so confirms his covenant, which he swore to your ancestors, as it is today."*

In this chapter, we'll explore three common categories of distractions—People, Places, and Things—and how they can quietly or sometimes blatantly disrupt your path to financial freedom.

Distractions: People

You've probably heard the saying: *"Show me your five closest friends, and I'll show you your future,"* or *"You are the average of the five people you spend the most time with."*

These phrases are true, especially when it comes to money habits. The people you spend time with have a huge influence on your financial behaviors. If you surround yourself with people who overspend, lack discipline, or prioritize instant gratification, their habits can easily rub off on you.

"I Made It" Syndrome

Let me be real—this was one of my biggest struggles when I began my financial freedom journey. I felt obligated to help family and friends. I had a six-figure career, lived in a beautiful suburban home, drove a luxury car, and enjoyed nice dinners and vacations. But with that success came an unspoken expectation, the obligation to "help" family members.

I don't know where this pressure came from, but I believed that saying "no" would make me seem like I had *"turned my back"* on my family or *"forgotten where I came from."* It wasn't until I realized that as long as I had debt, I didn't have any "extra" money to help family and friends. Every dollar was already promised to someone else—credit card companies, mortgage loan officers, car companies and more.

Learning to say "no" became a turning point in my financial journey. It wasn't easy. I often felt guilty; other times, I felt judged. But God reminded me that if I truly wanted to change my family's future and leave an inheritance for my children's children (*Proverbs 13:22*), I needed to make wiser decisions with my resources.

How to Avoid People-Based Money Distractions

1. **Evaluate Your Circle:** Are your closest friends and family encouraging you to build wealth, or are they pushing you toward impulse spending and debt? Find your financial tribe—people who share your goals.
2. **Set Boundaries:** Learn to say "no" with love and firmness. Politely decline invitations or financial requests that conflict with your goals.
3. **Communicate Your Goals:** Be transparent with your close circle about your financial goals. Ask them to hold you accountable and support your journey.

Distractions: Places

The places we frequent—both physically and online—can have a big impact on our finances.

For me, it was Marshalls and TJ Maxx—my retail kryptonite. What started as "just looking" often turned into impulse spending. Whether I was bored, looking for emotional relief, or needed a quick pick-me-up, retail therapy gave me a temporary dopamine hit—but hurting my wallet in the long run.

Stores are expertly designed to make you spend:

- "Limited-time offers" create urgency.
- Sales and clearance tags make you feel like you're saving money.
- Endcaps and checkout displays tempt you with last-minute purchases.

But those short-term highs are followed by long-term regret when the credit card statement arrives.

Online shopping is even more dangerous. The "one-click" checkout button removes emotional barriers to spending and targeted ads make it easy to buy things you didn't even know you wanted.

Let's not forget subscription services—streaming platforms, retail boxes, digital memberships. These tiny monthly charges seem harmless but can add up over time.

How to Avoid Place-Based Distractions

1. **Avoid Tempting Places:** If the mall or online shopping apps are your weakness, unsubscribe from marketing emails, delete shopping apps, and limit exposure.
2. **Audit Your Subscriptions:** Check your recurring expenses every few months. Cancel anything you're not using regularly.
3. **Set a Spending Limit:** Decide on a budget before spending and stick to it.

Distractions: Things

Our attachment to material possessions is one of the most subtle distractions in our financial lives.

We buy things—cars, clothes, gadgets—not because we need them, but because they give us a sense of status, security, or emotional relief. The key is understanding the difference between **wants** and **needs**:

- **Wants**: Optional luxuries that enhance comfort or pleasure. Designer bags, luxury cars, and the latest tech gadgets. These purchases are usually driven by emotion or social pressure.

- ☐ **Needs**: Essential for survival and well-being. Rent, groceries, utilities, healthcare. These are non-negotiable essentials.

Understanding Wants vs. Needs

- ☐ **Wants:** Designer bags, luxury cars, the latest tech gadget. These purchases are usually driven by emotion or social pressure.
- ☐ **Needs:** Rent, groceries, utilities, healthcare. These are non-negotiable essentials.

Matthew 6:19-21 reminds us: *"Do not store up for yourselves treasures on earth… For where your treasure is, there your heart will be also."*

God doesn't want us to live without joy or comfort, but He doesn't want us enslaved to debt because of misplaced priorities.

How to Keep "Things" in Check

1. **Focus on Needs, Not Wants:**
   Before making a purchase, ask:
   - ☐ *"Will this bring long-term value to my life or is it just a temporary distraction?"*
   - ☐ *"Is this purchase taking me closer to or further from my financial goals?"*

2. **Practice Delayed Gratification:**
   If it's not urgent, wait a few days before buying. Most impulse purchases lose their appeal over time.

Stay Focused on God's Promises

Distractions—whether people, places, or things—can derail your financial journey. But staying focused on God's promises will guide you back on track.

John 10:10 *says: "The thief comes only to steal and kill and destroy; I have come that they may have life and have it to the full."*

God's plan for your finances is freedom, abundance, and purpose.

Stay focused, stay disciplined, and trust God to lead you to the promised land of financial peace and freedom.

THE KINGDOM GUIDE TO FINANCIAL WISDOM & EMPOWERMENT

CHAPTER 6
Create a Freedom Plan

CHAPTER SIX
Create a Freedom Plan

How do you feel when you hear the word "budget"? For many, it stirs up feelings of restriction, anxiety, or even guilt. Words like *"tight," "limited," "broke,"* or just plain *"no"* might come to mind. If your upbringing didn't include healthy conversations about money, or if your financial journey has been a challenging one, it's easy to associate budgeting with something negative.

But here's the truth: a budget isn't about restriction—it's about freedom. It's about creating a clear, God-centered plan for your finances so you can live with intention, peace, and purpose. That's why I call it a **Freedom Plan** instead of a budget. A Freedom Plan minimizes distractions, maximizes potential, and empowers you to make faith-driven financial decisions that align with God's promises for your life.

In Matthew 6:24, Jesus says, *"No one can serve two masters. Either you will hate the one and love the other, or you will be devoted to the one and despise the other."* A Freedom Plan ensures that money serves you, not the other way around. When you give your money purpose and direction, you break free from the cycle of living paycheck to paycheck, accumulating debt, and carrying the weight of financial stress. A Freedom Plan isn't about deprivation—it's about clarity, purpose, and freedom to make choices that honor God and align with your financial goals.

Creating Your Freedom Plan

A Freedom Plan isn't a one-size-fits-all formula—it's a personalized approach rooted in your values, goals, and responsibilities. But before we dive into numbers and spreadsheets, we must start with the foundation: prayer, assessment, and directing your money.

1. Prayer: The First Step to Financial Freedom

Before you make a single financial decision in your Freedom Plan, invite God into your planning. Pray for wisdom, discernment, and strength to steward your resources well. Ask God to help you align your spending with His will and to provide clarity as you create your plan.

"Commit to the Lord whatever you do, and He will establish your plans."
— Proverbs 16:3

This isn't just about numbers—it's about aligning your financial habits with God's purpose for your life.

2. Assessment: Know Your Financial Reality

Before you can create a plan, you need to know exactly where you stand. This step involves three critical assessments: Income, Expenses, and Spending Habits.

a. Assess Your Income

- ☐ List all sources of income: your salary, side gigs, freelance work, rental income, or any other financial streams.
- ☐ Calculate your total monthly income.

This number is your starting point—it tells you what resources you're working with.

b. Assess Your Expenses

Expenses fall into three main categories:

- **Fixed Expenses:** Regular, unchanging payments (e.g., rent, mortgage, utilities, insurance).
- **Variable Expenses:** Fluctuating costs (e.g., groceries, gas, dining out, entertainment).
- **Debt Payments:** Monthly minimums or extra payments on loans, credit cards, or other debts.

Don't forget about occasional or yearly expenses like car registration, birthdays, or annual memberships. These costs need to be factored into your plan.

c. Assess Your Spending Habits

Go back at least **3 months** and review your bank statements, budgeting apps, or receipts. Pay close attention to:

- How much you spend on eating out.
- How much goes toward subscriptions.
- The little expenses that add up over time.

You might be surprised by where your money is actually going. Awareness is the first step to making meaningful changes.

3. Direct Your Money: Give Every Dollar a Job

One of my favorite quotes from John Maxwell is: *"A budget (Freedom Plan) is telling your money where to go instead of wondering where it went."*

When you direct your money intentionally, you gain control, reduce financial stress, and build a path toward your goals. Build your Freedom Plan based on your "after savings" income. Pay yourself first (savings and investments) before allocating money to bills or discretionary spending.

Here's a simple guideline:

- **10% Tithing** — Honor God with your first fruits.
- **20% Savings and Investing** — Build your emergency fund, contribute to retirement, and invest for the future.
- **50% Needs** — Cover your rent/mortgage, utilities, groceries, and essential bills.
- **20% Debt and Wants** — Pay down debt and allow some room for dining out, entertainment, or non-essential purchases.

These percentages can be adjusted based on your financial season. If you're aggressively paying down debt, you might allocate more to debt repayment.

Use a Zero-Based Budgeting Approach:

- Every dollar of your income gets assigned a job (tithing, saving, bills, debt repayment, discretionary spending).
- Your income minus your expenses should equal zero at the end of each month.

This approach ensures that no dollar is left unaccounted for, and every cent contributes to your financial goals.

- Review your Freedom Plan at the end of every month.
- Compare your actual spending with your planned budget.
- Make adjustments for unexpected expenses, bonuses, or changes in income.

Financial planning isn't static—it's a dynamic process that requires regular review and refinement.

4. Be Disciplined and Consistent

The hardest part of any financial plan isn't creating it—it's sticking to it. Discipline and consistency will determine your success.

- **Set Realistic Expectations:** Don't create overly restrictive budgets that set you up for failure.
- **Build Accountability:** Share your goals with a spouse, friend, or financial coach who can help you stay on track.
- **Use Tools and Technology:** Budgeting apps, calendar reminders, and automation can simplify the process.

Remember, it takes about **90 days** to truly get the hang of your Freedom Plan. Don't get discouraged if it feels messy at first—keep going, keep refining, and keep showing up.

If You're Married, Plan Together

Finances are one of the leading causes of conflict in marriages, but they don't have to be.

- **Dream together:** Go back to your "why" as a couple and create shared financial goals.
- **Communicate openly:** Be honest about spending habits, fears, and expectations.
- **Seek help if needed:** If finances are causing tension, seek support from a professional financial counselor or mentor.

"Can two walk together unless they are agreed?" — **Amos 3:3**

Contentment: The Key to Financial Tranquility

A Freedom Plan isn't about deprivation—it's about intentionality. It's about learning to live with **contentment**.

"I have learned to be content whatever the circumstances." — **Philippians 4:11-13**

My husband has a saying: **"Don't compete, don't compare, don't complain."**

When we stop chasing comparison and start living in contentment within God's provision, we discover true peace.

Your Freedom Plan

Your Freedom Plan is more than a financial strategy —it's about stewardship. It's about aligning your financial habits with God's Word and creating a life of purpose, generosity, and freedom.

Stay focused. Stay consistent. And most importantly, stay faithful to the journey.

This is your Freedom Plan. Own it. Live it. And watch God move mightily in your finances.

CHAPTER 7
Avoid and Destroy Debt

CHAPTER SEVEN
Avoid and Destroy Debt

The Weight of Debt

"Therefore, we also, since we are surrounded by so great a cloud of witnesses, let us lay aside every weight, and the sin which so easily ensnares us, and let us run with endurance the race that is set before us." — **Hebrews 12:1**

Debt is a weight—heavy, restrictive, and suffocating. If you've ever felt suffocated by bills, payments, and the endless grip of interest, know this: **you are not alone.** A 2023 study by Payroll.org reveals that **78% of Americans live paycheck to paycheck.**

But what does that really mean? Living paycheck to paycheck means that there's barely enough left after covering essentials like housing, food, and transportation. If a single paycheck is late or missed, the entire financial structure starts to crumble. This cycle leaves little room for saving for emergencies, investing for the future, or building a lasting financial legacy.

Today, debt has become more than common—it's expected. Many see it as an avoidable part of life and some even treat it as a rite of passage into adulthood. I once had a conversation with my millennial niece who said most in her generation accept debt as a part of life. The idea of being completely debt-free felt like an impossible dream.

I could relate. My journey with debt began with student loans. When I received my first loan repayment statement, I was shocked to see a repayment plan stretched over **ten years**. Ten years? Frustrated, I called Sallie Mae and asked, *"Why does it take so long to pay this off?"* The representative's response changed my perspective: *"You can pay it off early if you want."*

That simple yet profound sentence changed everything for me. It made me realize I didn't have to settle for the standard repayment plan of 10 years as my financial fate.

Unfortunately, many people never ask those questions. Instead, the focus is on the monthly payment, not the total cost. This mindset keeps people stuck, never fully experiencing the freedom God wants for them.

What the Bible Says About Debt

The Bible doesn't forbid borrowing outright, but it warns against the dangers of debt:

- **Proverbs 22:7:** *"The rich rules over the poor, and the borrower is servant to the lender."*
- **Romans 13:8:** *"Let no debt remain outstanding, except the continuing debt to love one another, for whoever loves others has fulfilled the law."*

Debt is not just a financial burden; it's spiritual. It steals our peace, diverts our focus, and limits our ability to live and give generously. Instead of using our resources to bless others or build God's Kingdom, debt forces us to funnel money to creditors.

But here's the truth: **Debt is not inevitable. It's a choice.**

A Culture of Debt: A Historical Perspective

Understanding how debt became normalized helps to see, it has not always been this way and it does not have to be a permanent part of life. America's relationship with debt began during the Revolutionary War when congressional leaders borrowed **$75 million** (from France and the Netherlands) to fund the fight for independence. After the war, Congress established the U.S. Treasury Department to manage the growing debt.

President Andrew Jackson did not believe in debt. Jackson famously referred to debt as a *"national curse" and in* 1835 he made a bold move—President Jackson paid off the nation's debt entirely. From 1835-1836, just one brief year, the United States became completely debt-free. However, in 1837 there was an economic downturn and with Jackson's presidential term complete, Congress rekindled its relationship with debt, and the United States has been in debt ever since.

For individuals, consumer debt as we know it did not exist until the early 20th century. Credit was an informal arrangement between merchants and regular customers, typically established through a handshake. That changed when Henry Ford introduced installment payments to make his Model T accessible. Soon, the idea spread to other businessmen and installment plans became widely available for furniture, refrigerators, and beyond.

Over time, borrowing became glorified. What was once labeled as shameful is now marketed as *"smart."* Financing has expanded to almost everything-even ear piercing.

The normalization is no accident. It's a tool the enemy uses to keep us enslaved, distracted, and unable to walk fully in God's purpose.

The Spiritual Side of Debt

Debt isn't just a financial issue; it's deeply spiritual. When we rely on loans and credit to meet our needs, we're bypassing God's timing and provision. Instead of waiting on Him, we trust lenders. But Philippians 4:19 reminds us: *"And my God will meet all your needs according to the riches of His glory in Christ Jesus."*

Breaking free from debt isn't just financial; it's an act of faith. When we align our money with God's principles, He opens doors and provides opportunities.

Destroying Debt: The Debt Snowball Method

Debt is a thief, **but you can take back what it has stolen. The Debt Snowball Method, popularized by Dave Ramsey, is one of the most effective tools to destroy debt.**

Here's how it works:

1. **List All Your Debts**
   Write down all your debts, from the **smallest balance to the largest.**
2. **Pay Minimums on All Debts**
   Make the minimum payments on all your debts so you stay current and avoid late fees.
3. **Attack the Smallest Debt**
   Throw every extra dollar you can at your smallest debt until it's gone.
4. **Celebrate Every Victory**
   Acknowledge your progress with each debt you eliminate. You've accomplished a goal and built some momentum.
5. **Roll the Payment into the Next Debt**
   Take the money you were putting toward the smallest debt and add it to the payment for the next smallest debt. Continue to pay the minimums on the others.

6. **Repeat the Process**
   Keep paying off debts one by one, rolling the payment amount into the next one each time.

Eventually, you will reach your largest debt. By then your "snowball" will be big and you will be able to make large payments to destroy your debt.

Faith and Financial Freedom

Debt repayment is more than a financial strategy—it's an act of **faith and obedience.**

- **Pray for wisdom:** *James 1:5* tells us to ask God for wisdom, and He will provide it.
- **Trust God's provision:** Remember He is your source, not your paycheck or credit card.
- **Stay consistent:** Pay down your debts faithfully, little by little, trusting that each step is bringing you closer to freedom.

The most critical step to breaking free from debt is simple but profound: **Stop borrowing money.**

- No more financing non-essentials.
- No more relying on credit cards.
- No more "Buy Now, Pay Later" plans.

Every dollar you borrow is a dollar that ties you to someone else's control. Debt doesn't have to define your story. With faith, discipline, and intentionality, you can break free!

- **Trust God with your finances.**
- **Use the Debt Snowball Method.**
- **Stay consistent and celebrate each victory.**

Let this be your declaration: **"I will no longer be a servant to debt. I will trust God, steward wisely, and walk in financial freedom."**

Your journey to freedom begins now. Step boldly into it with faith as your guide and God as your provider.

THE KINGDOM GUIDE TO FINANCIAL WISDOM & EMPOWERMENT

CHAPTER 8
Health is Wealth

CHAPTER EIGHT
Health is Wealth

Health: The Foundation of True Wealth

As a medical provider and a Believer, I would be remiss if I didn't address the biblical importance of health in the pursuit of financial prosperity. Too often, we overlook health when discussing success, but the Bible is clear: true wealth encompasses more than just money or material gain—it is deeply rooted in both physical and spiritual well-being. *"Beloved, I pray that you may prosper in all things and be in health, just as your soul prospers."* 3 John 1:2 (NKJV)

This scripture highlights an essential truth: God desires us to thrive in every area of life—spiritually, physically, and financially. Prosperity isn't confined to bank accounts and business ventures; it extends to the state of our health, our mental wellbeing, and our ability to serve God's purpose.

When we take care of our bodies—our most valuable earthly asset—we honor God's creation. Health equips us with the strength, vitality, and clarity to pursue His calling. Without it, even the most impressive financial achievements lose their meaning.

The Connection Between Health and Prosperity

The ability to earn, build wealth, and enjoy the fruit of our labor is a blessing from God, but it hinges on good health. When illness or physical limitations arise, productivity diminishes, financial stability wavers, and peace of mind becomes difficult to maintain.

Paul writes in 1 Corinthians 6:19-20: *"Do you not know that your bodies are temples of the Holy Spirit, who is in you, whom you have received from God? You are not your own; you were bought at a price. Therefore, honor God with your bodies."*

Our bodies are not just biological machines—they are sacred vessels entrusted to us by God. Caring for them isn't about vanity; it's an act of worship and stewardship.

This chapter isn't about fitness trends or diet fads—it's about honoring God by caring for the body He gave you, enabling you to live with purpose, vitality, joy, and strength.

Fueling the Temple: Nutrition Matters

We've all been there- indulging in an unhealthy food choice and saying *"I'm going to pay for this later."* Whether it's an extra donut, a sugary drink, or my personal favorite—a juicy burger with fries—our choices either fuel us or slow us down.

I was born diabetic, which shaped how I approach nutrition. From day one, my body endured trauma, and eating well is my way of thanking God for the gift of life. I'm not perfect—I still enjoy desserts now and then—but I know my limits and choose to respect them.

My mom taught me the power of nutrition when she was diagnosed with high cholesterol during my high school years. She came home, threw out the bacon grease, and declared, *"We're changing how we eat."* No more ribs, no more smothered pork chops—it felt like the end of the world. But her commitment paid off. Decades later, she manages her cholesterol through diet alone, without medication.

The lesson Is simple: **Your health is your responsibility.** You are what you eat. Fill your plate with leafy greens, lean proteins, and whole foods. Limit processed sugars and unhealthy fats. Teach your children these habits too. I have my daughters eating veggies for breakfast! They may not appreciate it now, but one day, they will.

Move Your Body: Exercise is Non-Negotiable

If you haven't felt your body breaking down yet, as my Grandma Lovie used to say, *"Just keep living."*

As a Physician Assistant in the Army, I spent years working long hours seeing 30 patients a day. After 22 years of military service, my body had endured a lot of trauma so I took time off to "rest." After a while my back began to ache, my joints were stiff and I felt decades older than I was. I thought something was wrong. Every test came back normal, and the truth was clear: I had simply stopped moving.

I knew I needed to stay active, but I no longer enjoyed running the standard 3-5 miles daily. I took the small step to begin walking during my lunch breaks. The warm sun, fresh air and body movement began the healing process. Motivated to decrease my aches and pains, I began searching for something that would fit into my new life as a civilian. I tried biking, Zumba, kickball, weightlifting and swimming but I just didn't find joy in the activities. One day I found something that worked for me: Christian Yoga. It combines movement, resistance, and meditation on scripture allowing me to honor my body without undue strain.

Here's the takeaway: Find what works for you—walking, dancing, yoga, weightlifting—and do it consistently. Your body was made to move. If you don't use it, you'll lose it.

Rest: God's Gift for Renewal

In our hustle-driven culture, rest can feel like a luxury. But rest isn't optional; it's essential. When we sleep, our bodies heal, our minds reset, and our immune systems strengthen. Sleep regulates hormones, clears toxins from the brain and body, and restores energy.

Psalm 116:7 reminds us *"Return to your rest, my soul, for the Lord has been good to you."*

Aim for 7-9 hours of sleep each night. And yes, naps count too. When you're well-rested, you make wiser decisions, think more clearly, and tackle challenges with resilience.

Manage Your Stress: Protect Your Peace

Stress is one of the leading causes of poor health. It can manifest as headaches, muscle tension, digestive issues, anxiety, and even heart problems.

I learned this the hard way when chronic stress caused me to develop severe heartburn. It wasn't until I read *Why Zebras Don't Get Ulcers* by Robert Sapolsky that I understood the toll stress takes on the body.

Philippians 4:6-7 became my lifeline: *"Do not be anxious about anything, but in every situation, by prayer and petition, with thanksgiving, present your requests to God. And the peace of God, which transcends all understanding, will guard your hearts and your minds in Christ Jesus."*

To manage stress, I:

- ☐ **Exercise regularly** (Christian Yoga).
- ☐ **Eat nutritious meals.**
- ☐ **Get adequate sleep.**
- ☐ **Set boundaries**
- ☐ **Take "me time" without guilt.**

Like paying yourself first financially, you must pay yourself first in self-care. You can't pour from an empty cup.

Stewardship and Health

The decisions you make about your health are acts of stewardship. Eating well, exercising, resting, and managing stress are vital.

When you prioritize your health:

- ☐ You honor God with your body.
- ☐ You increase your energy and productivity.
- ☐ You reduce long-term healthcare costs.
- ☐ You set an example for your family.

Psalm 91:16 assures us: *"With long life I will satisfy him and show him my salvation."*

God desires for you to live a long and abundant life —but that requires your participation. Health is wealth—not just because it keeps you productive, but because it enables you to live the life God designed for you. So, eat well, move your body, rest, and protect your peace.

Your health is a treasure—don't waste it.

CHAPTER 9
Faith Fueled Financial Living

CHAPTER NINE
Faith Fueled Financial Living

As we come to the close of this journey through biblical financial wisdom, it's important to remember that everything we've discussed—establishing your "why," setting financial goals, building savings, avoiding and eliminating debt, investing wisely, and giving generously—is more than a list of financial strategies. These are guiding principles for a life well-lived, one that aligns with God's purpose, reflects faithful stewardship, and overflows with generosity.
This journey isn't just about accumulating wealth; it's about creating a life of freedom, purpose, and alignment with God's will.

Believe God's Word

To experience the abundant life God desires for you, it is essential to believe and trust in His Word. The Bible teaches that God wants you to prosper in every area of life—emotionally, physically, mentally, spiritually, and financially. In 3 John 1:2, we are reminded that God desires for us to be in good health and to prosper just as our souls prosper. As believers, we are part of God's Kingdom, where there is no lack. Psalm 23:1 reassures us that, "The Lord is my shepherd; I shall not want," meaning, God will provide for all our needs. When we align our beliefs with His promises, we open ourselves to His abundant blessings.

Though living by God's Kingdom principles may feel counter to the world's thinking, we are called to trust in God's provision. The Bible promises that God is faithful to supply everything we need. Philippians 4:19 tells us He will provide for us according to His riches in glory. Trust that God will keep His promises—He is not a man that He should lie (Numbers 23:19). As you embrace His Word and trust Him, you will begin to see His blessings of prosperity, including financial provision, unfold in your life, just as He promises in Malachi 3:10 when He opens the windows of heaven for you.

Establishing Your "Why" — The Foundation of Financial Freedom

A key part of your financial journey is understanding your "why." Why do you want to manage your finances well? Is it to provide stability for your family, create opportunities for your community, or break generational cycles of financial struggle? Proverbs 16:3 reminds us, *"Commit to the Lord whatever you do, and he will establish your plans."*

When your "why" is deeply rooted in God's purpose for your life, your financial decisions become guided by His wisdom. This clarity fuels your focus, strengthens your discipline, and gives you the resolve to stay on course even when challenges arise. Your "why" isn't just a goal—it's your anchor.

Setting Financial Goals — A Vision for Your Future

Once your "why" is clear, the next step is to set financial goals. Proverbs 21:5 teaches us, *"The plans of the diligent lead to profit as surely as haste leads to poverty."*

Setting financial goals isn't just about building wealth—it's about crafting a roadmap to fulfill your God-given purpose. Goals provide direction and accountability.

Whether it's building an emergency fund, saving for your children's education, paying off your mortgage, or preparing for retirement, each goal moves you closer to financial freedom and Kingdom impact.

Be specific, measurable, and prayerful as you set your goals, knowing that God has equipped you with the strength and resources to accomplish them all.

Proverbs 6:6-8 gives us wisdom from an unexpected teacher—the ant. *"Go to the ant, you sluggard; consider its ways and be wise! It has no commander, no overseer or ruler, yet it stores its provisions in summer and gathers its food at harvest."*

Like ants, we are called to prepare for the seasons ahead. Having savings, especially in the form of an emergency fund, isn't just good financial advice—it's biblical wisdom.

Savings bring peace of mind, protect us from financial crises, and create space for generosity. Building a financial cushion is an act of obedience and trust, acknowledging God's provision and our responsibility to steward it wisely.

Avoiding Debt — A Biblical Warning

Debt is one of the most significant financial burdens we can carry. Proverbs 22:7 warns us, *"The rich rule over the poor, and the borrower is servant to the lender."*

Debt limits your freedom. It steals your peace. It hinders your ability to live generously.

While borrowing may sometimes be an option, it must be approached with wisdom and caution. Avoid debt for fleeting desires or temporary pleasures. Instead, focus on living within your means, practicing contentment, and honoring God with every dollar you earn.

Getting Out of Debt — Freedom in Christ

If you're already in debt, don't lose hope. Financial restoration is possible with God's guidance and your commitment to change.

Proverbs 3:5-6 encourages us, *"Trust in the Lord with all your heart and lean not on your own understanding; in all your ways submit to him, and he will make your paths straight."*

Start with prayer, seek wisdom, and create a clear debt repayment plan. Use the debt snowball, make sacrifices where needed, and stay focused on your goals.

Every payment you make isn't just reducing debt—it's reclaiming your freedom.

Investing is a God-idea, Ecclesiastes 11:2 advises, *"Invest in seven ventures, yes, in eight; you do not know what disaster may come upon the land."*

Diversify your investments. Plan for the long term. Whether it's retirement accounts, real estate, or other opportunities, let your money grow intentionally.

But remember—your ultimate security doesn't come from your investments. It comes from God, who is your true provider.

Giving Generously — The Heart of a Faithful Steward

Generosity is at the core of faith-fueled financial living. Acts 20:35 reminds us, *"It is more blessed to give than to receive."*

When we give, we acknowledge that everything we have belongs to God and our generosity is just a reflection of our God-like character.

Your giving can change lives. It can feed the hungry, shelter the homeless, support ministries, and inspire hope. Giving freely and joyfully not only blesses others but also deepens your faith and trust in God's provision.

The Bigger Picture

Financial stewardship is about living a life that reflects God's heart. Proverbs 22:6-7 gives us this instruction: *"Train up a child in the way they should go, and when they are old, they will not depart from it. The rich rule over the poor, and the borrower is servant to the lender."*

Our financial decisions ripple into the lives of our children, grandchildren, and communities. What legacy are you building? Are you setting a foundation of faith, wisdom, and generosity?

True financial success isn't measured by bank statements or material possessions—it's measured by how well we honor God with what He has given us.

As you reflect on your financial journey, remember that every decision you make is an opportunity to honor God. Financial freedom isn't a final destination—it's an ongoing journey of faith, discipline, and trust.

Proverbs 3:9-10 offers this encouragement: *"Honor the Lord with your wealth, with the first fruits of all your crops; then your barns will be filled to overflowing, and your vats will brim over with new wine."*

Trust God with your resources. Seek His wisdom in every financial decision. And remember, your finances are not just about you—they're about building God's Kingdom, blessing others, and living out your God-given purpose.

As you close this chapter, let these truths sink deeply into your heart:

- ☐ Your financial journey is a spiritual journey.
- ☐ God desires you to prosper—not just financially, but in every area of your life.
- ☐ Faith, discipline, and obedience are the keys to lasting financial freedom.

May your financial life be a reflection of God's grace, wisdom, and faithfulness. Keep your eyes fixed on Him. Walk boldly in faith. And trust that as you honor God with your resources, He will honor you abundantly. This isn't the end of your financial journey—it's just the beginning of something extraordinary.

Faith Fueled FINANCE$

KINGDOM GUIDE TO FINANCIAL WISDOM & EMPOWERMENT

VERONICA ALSTON

About The Author
VERONICA ALSTON

About The Author
VERONICA ALSTON

Veronica Alston is a dynamic thought leader in biblical finance, dedicated to guiding countless believers toward financial freedom through the transformative power of biblical principles. A passionate educator and mentor, she has made an indelible mark as a guest lecturer at high schools, colleges, and universities, as well as through her active participation in financial literacy programs within her local community.

Veronica also brings her expertise to Raleigh North Christian Center in Raleigh, North Carolina, where she teaches financial education rooted in faith. Her ability to bridge the gap between spiritual and practical financial management has empowered individuals and families to break free from debt and live purpose-filled lives aligned with God's plan.

Born in Kansas City, Missouri, Veronica now resides in Rolesville, North Carolina, with her husband, CW2 (Ret.) Dan T. Alston, affectionately known as "Chief," and their two beautiful girls, Olivia and Lauryn. Her journey of faith, perseverance, and disciplined financial growth is a testament to her teachings.

A proud graduate of Financial Peace University and a trained financial coach through Dave Ramsey's program, Veronica combines her personal experience and professional training to inspire and equip others. Her 22 years of service in the United States Army shaped her resilience and commitment to excellence.

In addition to her financial expertise, Veronica holds a Master of Science degree and serves as a practicing Physician Assistant, specializing in natural and regenerative medicine. Her diverse skills and unwavering faith make her a beacon of hope and transformation for those seeking to align their finances with their spiritual purpose.

Through her book, *Faith-Fueled Finances*, Veronica invites readers to embark on a journey toward financial freedom, blending timeless biblical wisdom with actionable strategies for a life of abundance, purpose, and faith.

Faith Fueled FINANCE$

AN KINGDOM GUIDE TO FINANCIAL WISDOM & EMPOWERMENT

READY TO WALK IN FINANCIAL FREEDOM, CONTACT COACH VERONICA:
VLYNNALSTON@GMAIL.COM

VERONICAALSTON.COM

shero.
Publishing

Made in the USA
Middletown, DE
08 February 2025

70957873R10071